This book is for you if you...

- are Super Rich and want to protect your money from risks, cheats and crooks; excessive taxation, undisclosed professional fees, protracted litigation, disgruntled heirs, estranged family members, divorced spouses, clever con men and false friends – who can you trust?

- want to find advisers you can Trust – your 'Ring of Confidence'

- want to manage your 'Ring of Confidence' – your Trusted Advisers; not let them manage you

- are working with or for the Super Rich* – you need to know what it is like being Super Rich and understand why they sometimes behave irrationally

- want to be Super Rich so that you can start to plan now

- want insights into the lives of the Super Rich

*If you are working with the Super Rich and want to know *'How to win business from the Private Client – uncovering the secrets'* you may want to buy our book. This can be bought direct from **www.garnhamfos.com**

Caroline Garnham

About the author

Caroline Garnham, a former leading private client lawyer and head of Simmons & Simmons private client practice for fifteen years, was nominated as one of the top five leading private client lawyers by *The Lawyer* in 2011. She was a contributor for the *Financial Times* for twelve years, pioneered the area of law now known as Family Governance and proposed and drafted the Executive Entity Act for the Bahamas, which became law in December 2011.

This book draws on her extensive knowledge and intimate experience in working for some of the world's wealthiest families. Pulling together scores of examples she looks at the relationship of the UHNW community with their advisors.

It is often overlooked that the Super Rich give most to our economy, and to the lives of ordinary people through their entrepreneurial endeavors. But the rich are a minority, and one of the few groups where prejudice flourishes. It is fair game to invade their privacy, expose their weaknesses and publish their private financial data. In many cases, this is an abuse of power about which very little is being done.

Caroline is still very active in the private client world as an adviser to some of the wealthiest families. She is able to cater to their needs independently through Garnham Family Office Services.

She finds that the top five needs and concerns of this hard to reach rich minority are usually very similar. Mainly, they want to be in control of their wealth – they cannot hope to know everything, so it is important they know how to pick trusted advisers, remove and replace those who let them down and have the right tools to manage their inner Ring of Confidence.

They also look for a club of peers with whom they can network and learn from. BConnect Club is an exclusive Club for UHNW Individuals which connects them to other wealthy families, professional information, exclusive luxury products and investment opportunities. UHNW families join the network for free subject to a verification process that they are worth in excess of a minimum of £5million. Those interested in co-investing can find projects and ventures pre-screened for their benefit, they can also attend the launch of luxury products and find the relevant information they need to stay on top of their wealth and their inner Ring of Confidence.

BConnect Club provides a safe and secure neutral platform, where they can find information relevant to their circumstances and requirements, new luxury products and exclusive investment opportunities.

If you are Super Rich and want to be part of our Club, speak to specialists, introduce the second generation to the world of managing wealth, or simply want a source of independent information you can sign up to Caroline's free weekly blog on
http://www.garnhamfos.com/notes-from-caroline/

Is trust the one thing that money cannot buy?

So who can you trust when you are super rich?

If you don't manage your advisors they will manage you

By Caroline Garnham

Published by
Filament Publishing Ltd
16, Croydon Road, Waddon, Croydon,
Surrey, CR0 4PA, United Kingdom
Telephone +44 (0)20 8688 2598
Fax +44 (0)20 7183 7186
info@filamentpublishing.com
www.filamentpublishing.com

ISBN - 978-1-910125-40-3

Printed by IngramSpark

Contents

This book is for you if you...   1

About the author   3

Foreword   9

Introduction   11

Chapter 1: Goal setting for UHNWs   15

Chapter 2: Planning for UHNWs   35

Chapter 3: Time management for UHNWs   51

Chapter 4: Getting there: UHNWs   69

Chapter 5: Getting more: UHNWs   85

Chapter 6: UHNWs: delivery   103

Chapter 7: Retain and maintain: UHNWs   121

Chapter 8: Trust and advisors: UHNWs   137

Book Extras   153

Ring of Confidence   155

BConnect Club   157

Foreword

I never thought I would feel sorry for the super rich. Caroline Garnham has exposed "the other side of the coin", in identifying the issues they face of knowing whom they can trust to advise them; being fingered or pestered for money all the time; being super-taxed by the Government and often criticised for their success and told to pay more tax by politicians.

Caroline's book is about how the super rich should manage their lives and manage their affairs, providing a down-to-earth, practical platform.

Her book rests on the fact that, constructively, our society generates new self-made individuals, always the result of endeavour and hard work, but often coming as a surprise to the individuals in question who need to learn how to manage and what to do with their wealth and how to select advisers.

The book contains an interesting review of the Family Office option as well as the full range of investment assets and their limitations.

In short, this is a book which every self-made successful individual should read and digest – preferably before they cash in their fortunes!

The Lord Flight

Introduction

Chapter summary:

- Billionaires oil the wheels of the economy, leading countries out of recession.

- UHNW individuals are tired of being poorly served by advisors with an eye to their own pockets rather than your needs.

- Your worries need to be addressed by advisors you can trust – but where do you find them?

Working as a private client lawyer for more than twenty years, I have developed a sympathy for you, the Ultra High Net Worth community. You may not have to worry about a mortgage or where the next meal is coming from, but you do have your own concerns, which need to be understood to be served. You contribute significantly in taxes which benefits us all; in Great Britain the top 1% pay 30% of our income tax, you spend in our shops and oil the wheels of our economy – however, in general you are poorly served and often despised.

This book *So who can you trust when you are super rich?* is designed for you, the super rich and those aspiring to be super rich. If having too little money used to keep you awake at night, what are your worries now that you have too much? This book will tell you how to manage your advisors who are your Ring of Confidence, your wealth and how to enjoy it.

As UHNW individuals I understand you are being fingered for money ALL THE TIME. It is hardly surprising therefore that you fly off the handle when you are being fleeced for yet more. Being pestered for money is a way of life for you and most of you hate it which is why you want to preserve your privacy.

People who are not as wealthy as you watch your frustrations with surprise, but they do not know what it is like being wealthy while you do.

What UHNWs want

You are sick of being used like an ATM, which means you are looking for people you can trust. But trustworthy people cannot be bought with money – that is to do with attitude. You want advisors who care for you, who see you as people rather than money-mountains. The government is guilty of this too: debates continue as to whether you should pay more, because you have more. But *why* should you pay more than half of everything you earn just because the government says that there are people in the country who are less well off? You pay VAT on everything you buy, capital gains tax on every investment you sell at a profit, and huge amounts of income tax not only on the income you make, but also on the wages of the people you employ and the businesses you bring into this country with you.

You have also told me that you want to meet people like you. Very often, one of the first things people do when they become wealthy is to start looking for private members' clubs to join in order to network with 'those like them' – those who may have similar concerns and those who actually might hold the answers to your problems. We have taken the idea of networking with likeminded people a step further by creating the BConnect Club. It is a platform where our members can come together to discuss their concerns, talk about what interests them, inspire the younger generation to be proactive, co-invest with others, meet each other and feel better in control of your wealth empire.

From our discussions, and in particular with in-depth talks with Charles, Tom, John, Christina, James, Ed, Philip and many others, you told me what you wanted.

So we created a platform that would:

- Preserve your privacy. At **www.bconnectclub.com** you'll find all you need and want to know about investing, spending and giving your wealth.

- Help you avoid making mistakes. Here you can learn from the experts on how to manage your wealth, find luxury products, and enjoy yourself without revealing who you are or in what you may be interested.

- Provide you with convenience. You wanted everything you needed to know about spending, investing and giving wealth in one place at one time.

- Help the next generation feel inspired to learn about business, managing wealth, managing advisors and make sure they are prepared to step into your shoes.

- Give you the information you need, while sparing you the information you don't. We do this by including a 'follow' functionality. The news, views or case studies of any advisor or purveyor of luxury goods, if 'followed', will be filtered onto your home page. (Please note however that this facility does not work unless you are registered).

- Give feedback to advisors and luxury purveyors. We did this by including a 'like' button.

- Make it easy for you to share something of interest with your family, friends and contacts. We did this by including a 'share' facility which again only works if you are registered and logged in.

UHNWs are good for the economy

I firmly believe that you, the Ultra High Net Worth community, can between you save the world and our economy. You have already made a major impact on the economy of Britain. But to make a difference worldwide you need advisors and luxury goods purveyors who understand you and what you want, which inspired me to write the book Uncovering the secrets to winning business from private clients. It is accompanied by Educational Notes, Video and Questionnaires so that you, or your Advisor can learn through the eight step guide how to win business and trust.

If you are an UHNW individual or an advisor and would like to find out more go to **www.bconnectclub.com**.

Chapter 1
Goal setting for UHNWs

Chapter summary:

- Ultra High Net Worth (UHNW) individuals need advisors they can trust.

- Self-made UHNWs are most vulnerable in the first five years following their liquidity event.

- The importance of managing liquid wealth.

- Tools for UHNWs: the asset audit.

- Tools for UHNWs: goal setting for investing, spending and giving.

Self-made UHNWs value trust

Most Ultra High Net Worth (UHNW) individuals are self made and are looking for people to trust. Joanne Rowling, better known as JK Rowling, sold nearly 500 million books that told the story of Harry Potter, a boy wizard. The books were made into eight films which netted £5 billion at the box office. But Joanne was not born with a silver spoon in her mouth. She was born in Yate, near Bristol, and was a single mother living hand-to-mouth in Edinburgh when her first Harry Potter book came out in 1997.

According to the Sunday Times' rich list 2014, Joanne Rowling now ranks as the UK's 180th wealthiest person. She has a net worth of £570 million, 50% more than the Queen, whose net wealth is estimated at £330 million. The difference, however, between the Queen and JK Rowling is that the Queen was born into wealth whereas Joanne had it thrust upon her.

John Caudwell, with a net worth in excess of £1.5 billion, made his money through Phones 4u. He grew up in poverty in Stoke on Trent and now lives in a mansion in Mayfair.

Duncan Bannatyne started out selling ice creams from a van.

Self-made Ultra High Net Worth individuals did not learn the intricacies of wealth management from childhood nor inherit their advisors along with their family's riches. Furthermore, they will not have made the sort of contacts and friends through school or university who could guide them. Most do not know where to start in managing their wealth on their first liquidity event.

The wealthy are a minority group. There is very little written advice available to them on how to make the right decisions about their money and find the right investment opportunities. They do not know who to trust. Although most people believe that the wealthy are privileged with advisors telling them how to avoid tax and make their millions go further, in truth, UHNW individuals find it just as hard to find good advisors as it is for good advisors to find clients.

The curse of new wealth

Many of our new rich struggle in the first few years after a liquidity event; often plagued by feelings of guilt and disbelief, as well as feeling isolated, lonely and out of their depth.

Gary Barlow of Take That nearly lost his OBE and certainly damaged his reputation by investing in Ice Breaker, a film scam.

But how was he to know that the investment was not approved by HMRC? How was he to know that he was being mis-sold a tax scheme? People with experience, like Howard Raymond, King of Soho, would not touch such investments with a barge pole, but he is second generation and 'knows these things'.

> ...'a fool and his money are soon parted' is very true, except that the UHNW new into liquid wealth does not know how to avoid being a fool.

Samantha (not her real name) won a million pounds in the lottery and for a while it ruined her life: she felt she did not deserve it, had no one to share it with, felt she was only liked for her good fortune and became a recluse as a result.

That is until she met Roger who had similar wealth and introduced her to new people and places. He taught her how to enjoy her wealth and what to do with it. She was lucky – most people meet others who are skilled at separating them from their money – 'a fool and his money are soon parted' is very true, except that the UHNW individual new into liquid wealth does not know how to avoid being a fool.

But it is not only people who sell their businesses or win the lottery who feel overwhelmed; this anxiety is also felt by people who inherit unexpected wealth, or valuable assets, or receive a fortune on a divorce.

Before the liquidity event, each of them knew their world and the rules that defined it, but after it those rules no longer apply. Like Alice falling down the rabbit hole into Wonderland, one moment everything was known and fine and the next everything had changed completely; people respond differently towards you, expect more from you and you can now do things your friends cannot, which leads to feelings of estrangement and isolation. I call this kind of anxiety 'mortgages to management': one moment you are looking at the interest rate and wanting it to be as low as possible and the next you look at it and wanting it to be as high as possible.

If you are an Ultra High Net Worth individual, the only difference between you and everyone else is that you have wealth and most people don't. Wealth requires decisions to be made, and in making these decisions you need advisors. But who do you trust?

Most people say you should trust your instincts, but in the majority of cases people don't begin to trust them until they have made mistakes, which, if you are a UHNW, means losing money; in some cases, all of your money. The intention of this book is not only to provide insights into the world of the wealthy, but also to help UHNWs understand the world of advisors. After all, if advisors are to change it is up to clients to make that happen.

When are UHNW individuals at their most vulnerable?

Just like a butterfly is at its most vulnerable for the first few hours after emerging from the chrysalis, UHNWs are at their most vulnerable for the first five years following a liquidity event.

They are easy prey for anyone seeking funds; the equity project 'that will make a fortune', the charity that feeds on guilt, they're told they need to avoid tax, plan for succession with trusts, family constitutions, manage their wealth with discretionary portfolio management – the list is endless. The ideal time to take advice is a couple of years BEFORE a liquidity event – to avoid being bamboozled afterwards.

> The ideal time to take advice is a couple of years BEFORE a liquidity event – to avoid being bamboozled afterwards.

When I was head of the private client group at Simmons & Simmons a colleague introduced me to Bob (not his real name) with the words "I don't know what Caroline does, but you need to see her." Bob was the co-owner of a very successful business which he was considering selling. The first thing I asked him was why he wanted an exit? If he were to hold on to the company it would be free of inheritance tax on his death which meant that he could pass the family wealth onto his children free of tax. He said he was fed up with working and wanted to sell the business. He understood the tax consequences and was clear that he wanted an exit.

I explained the mortgages to management anxiety to him. How leaving the business that he knew so well would mean entering a new and alien world. I advised him to find out as much as he could about managing family wealth and gave him the titles and authors of a few good books to get him started.

Next we went through his dreams and nightmares and the questions that I have set out below (see pages 19-25). We also discussed whether and to what extent he wanted to bring his family into the decision-making process. Then we went through the different options for managing his money and met with a variety of wealth managers. Finally we worked on his vision statement. Then all this work was shelved until two years later he was made an offer he could not refuse – tax or no tax – and he made a seamless and enjoyable transition from 'mortgages to management'.

Clogs to clogs in three generations

Every country has an expression like clogs to clogs, rice fields to rice fields, and rags to rags in three generations. In 1918 *Forbes* first published its list of the richest people in America, now nearly 100 years later and three or four generations on, not one of these families is in the top one hundred.

There are many reasons for this: taxes, dilution of capital through the growing family, expensive disputes, excessive spending, and disasters, but at the root is a failure to set goals and seek good advice. If you want wealth to remain in the family for longer than three generations, then you need to set your goals and act accordingly.

What can you do with money?

There are only three things you can do with wealth:

- **Invest it**,

- **Spend it**, or

- **Give it away** – which includes succession on death.

Of course, there is overlap; impact investing is a hybrid between philanthropy and investing, spending, say, on art, can be an investment, and you can spend on your children which can be classed as both spending and giving.

However, in general terms there are just three categories and these each need to be looked at and considered as part of a plan or strategy.

The first thing to remember is that there is no right or wrong; it is your money and you can do what you want with it. If your decision is to squander it – backing a three legged horse at Newbury races – that is fine, but you need to know what you are doing and face the consequences. Wealth, once it has been spent, given away or lost, is gone, it does not come back unless you are a serial entrepreneur and can make another fortune.

But it is not just about having or not having wealth and deciding what to do with it, there are sometimes unexpected implications and most of them involve people.

Managing the people who manage the money

It is not just the money; it is managing the people you hire to look after it. If you have five houses each with a full complement of staff and in two of them you spend only four or five weeks a year, it is not just what those four/five weeks are costing you several

> It's not just about managing the money; it's also about managing the people you hire to look after it.

millions of pounds a year, but what your staff is doing for the ten months or so you are not there.

Consider the expression 'idle hands make light work'. Let us imagine Marcos, the head butler of a house in the South of France. His employer Margaret spends only four weeks a year in her French home. Marcos is about to turn 50, it is February, when Margaret is in Florida. Juliette the French cook decides to 'borrow' a bottle of Petrus to celebrate his birthday. It is delicious. A few weeks later, no one has spotted the missing bottle, so Marcos and Juliette decide to borrow another bottle of Petrus. By the time it comes to the fifth bottle a few months later, they no longer feel guilty and start to excuse their bad behaviour by bad-mouthing Margaret: "Stupid drunk, she'll never notice a few missing bottles." This sort of rot, if left unchecked, can extend to other items and objects.

I once knew an elderly woman called Cynthia, who shared her home with Nancy, a full-time domestic nurse. Cynthia was not in the best of health. One evening, I noticed Nancy was wearing one of her employer's brooches as she was going out. When I quizzed her, she said that her employer had said she could wear it. When Cynthia died, I was curious to note that the brooch was not amongst her possessions. I asked Nancy about it and she said that Cynthia had given her the brooch, but there was nothing in writing to back up her claim.

Whether you like it or not, wealth needs to be managed and you need to manage those people you employ to do so.

Wealth suffers from entropy. If you do not put in the time and energy to look after it and the people you engage, one day you will wake up and it will be gone. If you have a garden seat, you need to sand it down and lacquer it on a regular basis, if not it will eventually deteriorate and fall apart. So it is with wealth. If you are not on top of it and know what you are doing with it, it will start to diminish, and once lost, rarely can you get it back.

Where are you and what are you doing?

Before you decide where you want to go with your wealth and the people you need to engage to help you, you need to know where you are. The majority of clients I have worked with over the years are extraordinarily casual about their wealth and the people they engage to look after it, once it is in liquid form. They may have been fastidious when they were running their business, but the moment it turns into cash, discipline disappears. Most records of assets are kept on spreadsheets, if kept at all, even if managed by a family office. There are umpteen computer programmes that can provide real time reports as well as projections, but 80% don't use them.

However you keep track of your wealth it is important to know what you have and who is managing it for you. If you have not done an asset audit this is where you need to start.

The problem is that it involves keeping a check on what you are spending and most people do not like doing this.

Imagine your wardrobe and cupboards at home: do you know what is in them? You may have trousers you haven't worn, shirts and blouses hung, but forgotten about. Now multiply that by one thousand – the UHNW individual can buy more, but they do not always know what they have, and for many keeping a record is boring. But it really does need to be done if you want to make the most of what you have.

What does an asset audit look like?

If you were a company, your Balance Sheet would show:

- **Your fixed assets**. What you cannot sell – your home, chattels and art for example.

- **Your current assets**. What is funding your everyday living expenses – you can call these your 'lifestyle investments'.

- **Your current liabilities**. What you need to pay – cost of staff, investment managers, utility bills, and,

- **Your capital and reserves**. What you have over and above your lifestyle investments – these can be called your 'legacy investments'.

Then you have your Profit and Loss account:

- **Turnover.** What is coming in and where it's coming from.

- **Less cost of sales.** What is being paid to get this, dealing costs, taxes and so on.

- **Less expenses.** What you are actually spending.

There are lots of people who can help you do an audit and run a software program that can manage your assets and liabilities. You just need to do it and do it in a disciplined and methodical manner.

As soon as you know where you are you can start finding where you want to be. You then need to work out who you need to help you to get where you need to go.

I was talking to a professional trustee/private banker recently who said that if his clients spent even half the time and energy on running their private investments as they did on their company they would be a lot better off and would not waste so much time and valuable resources.

Understanding human nature

In their analysis of investor attitudes over the last few decades, behavioural scientists have noticed that investors react more strongly to losses than they do to gains. This is hardly surprising when you think about it.

Jon, a wealth manager, also appears on the rich list. In his opinion losses must be avoided at all costs. Why? If you make a loss, it is almost impossible to make it up again, let alone maintain a good return on what you have left. When it is gone, it is gone!

We are seeing a shift in professional investment management away from Modern Portfolio Theory to a Family Goal Based Investment

Strategy. In my opinion, this is great, because it puts the client back at the centre of the investment process. But before letting your advisor take too great a part in setting your goals – one word of warning.

An investment manager will have goals of his own and one of them will be to have 'assets under management'. If your strategy is to spend your money before you die, your goal and his goal will not be aligned. The same is true of any advisor; an investment manager will want to preserve your wealth, a trust lawyer will want you to put your wealth into a trust for future generations, and a yacht broker will want you to sell your yacht to buy an even more expensive one.

It is sensible first to have some idea of what YOU WANT before letting any advisor loose on your dreams and nightmares.

I know many UHNW people who have a healthy attitude towards their wealth, which is "I worked very hard to make it, so now I am going to work very hard to enjoy it. I have given the kids a good start, a good education, but now they need to make their own way in life. They should not expect anything from me on my death." This attitude is perfectly fine, but most advisors will try to talk you out of it by making you feel guilty for having such an hedonistic attitude.

Fanciful dreams or a living nightmare?

My area of expertise as a private client lawyer was Family Governance. This focuses on the distribution of power, especially where there is a family business, family home or priceless art collection. I likened it to the shift from 'benign dictatorship to democracy'. Governance sets out the rules on when and how a decision would be made, making sure that all interested parties were involved.

To give an example. Jacob had built a fortune and was passionate about his foundation which was dedicated to helping children in need whether in emerging markets or at home. He had three children who lived in their father's shadow. Jacob, without realising it, had made them feel inadequate. They felt they did not deserve the yachts, private planes and lavish events. They showed interest in his foundation, but in reality were feckless and lazy.

On their father's death, they continued to work for his foundation but as the years passed allowed the monies to accumulate without making many distributions. Jacob should have arranged for a tried and tested advisory board and a distribution policy to avoid non-distribution. He had the fanciful notion that his children, once he was no longer there, would somehow work together to live his dream to make vulnerable children's lives more tolerable, but they had neither the drive nor the inclination to make it happen and so did very little by way of charitable work.

Reality check

Not all founders want their children to work together, and some siblings just cannot. Realities need to be recognized, understood and accounted for.

Arun had a substantial business and all his wealth was tied up in it. On his sudden and unexpected death his daughter Tasha took over the day-to-day management of the business with her husband Asi. They worked hard and grew the business. Tasha's sisters, who were equal shareholders, did not work in the business. They complained that Tasha was paying herself and her husband a high salary and bonus which was prejudicing their interests as shareholders. They wanted Tasha and Asi to accept a reduced salary so that there would be more for them by way of returns on their shares.

Inevitably Tasha's sisters hired lawyers and tried to have Tasha and Asi removed as directors. This led to an expensive dispute and, as Tasha fought her sisters, the business declined.

Eventually it was decided to go to mediation and it ended up with Tasha buying out her sisters with the help of a bank loan secured on the assets of the business and Tasha's own home. This family dispute caused their mother much heartache because her daughters could no longer bear to be in the same room and were constantly critical of each other.

The second generation: workers or spenders?

Whether a child is able to work in a business, or indeed at anything, very often depends on how old they were when the founder had a liquidity event or became liquid wealthy.

From my experience, if children grow up watching their father and mother struggle and fight to build a business, they grow up wanting to work and improve upon what their parents have built. However, if children grow up in an environment of luxury, where they see their parents enjoying the fruits of their labour, they have no role model for hard work and tend to grow up self-centred, attention-seeking and lazy.

If a founder had children with one spouse before he became wealthy and more children with a new wife after making his fortune, seeds of disharmony will inevitably have been sown. In a situation like this it is almost impossible for the children to work together. The older siblings will be workers, the others spenders – poles apart. Of course, there are exceptions to this generalization, but it is often the case.

Privacy

UHNW individuals used to be called Private Clients. The less known about how much wealth they had the happier they were; the less they would be pestered or nagged for money. In most cases, the whingers were spend thrift children charities and opportunistic creditors.

Very often a family would protect their assets by transferring them into a trust. The trustees then protect the assets, like a hen on her brood of chicks. However, a much nastier predator is at the nest, the taxman. Governments have long been frustrated about the lack of information they have about their residents' wealth offshore, whether in trust or personally owned.

This is about to change as from 2017 nearly all governments around the world have complied with an OECD initiative to collate the financial information of financial assets held in their country and exchange it with the government of the country in which the owner is a tax payer. Jo, for example, has homes in London, Buenos Aires and Cape Town and bank accounts in Switzerland held by a trust in Jersey. Jo is fully tax compliant so why should he be worried? Jersey will collate all the financial information from his Jersey trustee together with the name of his Protector and anyone else who has significant influence.

The governments of Argentina, the UK and South Africa are all eager to make more revenue and have deep pockets to do so.

Most governments can make more revenue if it can prove the trust does not exist.

The doctrine of sham, hinges on the intention of the settlor at the time the trust was created and funded – did he mean to set up a trust and comply with its obligation. If he reserved too much power to himself at the time or to his Protector the trust can be set aside.

If a court endorses the claim that the trust be set aside governments can charge the settler to tax on all the income and gains made by the trust since inception, and the trustees will be made to pay back their fees.

The conundrum is how can a tax authority decide whether tax is being evaded, or a trust is real or a sham, unless it has all relevant information, and how does it collate this information without breaching the human rights to privacy?

In Article 8 European Convention on Human Rights, everyone can expect respect of privacy and family life, but this is qualified by the need of a country to look after the economic well-being of its residents. Currently financial information is automatically exchanged without much consideration as to whether there is a reasonable risk of tax evasion. Exactly where to draw the line between the need to collect taxes and the right to privacy will no doubt be aired in the European Court of Justice, but currently where the line should be drawn is blurred.

The erosion of privacy for the international UHNW family is the one biggest concern facing UHNW individuals at the time of writing, which is why UHNW families are seeking ways to avoid tax investigations, protect their privacy and preserve their assets. To do this they need advisers they can trust – their inner Ring of Confidence who need to meet and advise on a regular basis and not just when the UHNW family feels it is appropriate – which may then be too late. UHNW clients must be fully tax compliant, but to do so they need to know the rules which are rarely logical and have nothing to do with good intentions. Just because secrecy has become synonymous with tax evasion should not be the excuse to ride rough shod over Privacy.

Goal setting

An individual who has a liquidity event, whether on a divorce, death, or sale of a business, invariably loses sight of the fact that it is just as hard to manage liquid wealth as it is to run a business. For those who have become wealthy on divorce or through inheritance, they may never have run a business and will be at a disadvantage to those who have.

When wealth is liquid you need to set just as many goals as you would if you were running a business.

Wealth is like fire: it can give warmth, create light, and provide comfort, but only if it has the parameters of a hearth or boiler. If it has no boundaries it can destroy absolutely.

Setting goals is all about **being SMART**. SMART is the acronym for setting goals. They must be:

S	Specific
M	Measurable
A	Achievable
R	Relevant, and
T	Timely.

Take each of the three areas in which wealth can be deployed; investing, spending, and giving, and make a SMART map by answering the following questions.

Specific

Investing

Make a list of all your assets and investments.

- If you cannot – you are planning to lose them! Get an audit (see pages 16-17).

- Do you wish to continue holding each and every one?

- What are the returns on each asset and investment?

- Do you like this investment? Does it justify less than average performance?

- Who is assisting you in your investments? Are they any good?

- Do you like them?

- Should you switch advisors?

Spending

- Do you know how much you spend and on what?

- If not, do an audit and find out (see step two if you do not know how).

- Do you wish to continue this level of spending?

- Do you enjoy spending this money?

- Are there risks attached to spending money in this way and what are they?

- Who is assisting you in your spending and are they any good?

- Do you like them?

- Should you think of switching your advisors?

Giving (whether to charity or children)

- Do you wish to continue your existing level of giving?

- Do you enjoy this giving?

- Are there risks attached to this giving? What are they?

- What are the benefits you want from your giving?

- What benefits are you currently getting?

- Who is assisting you?

- Are they any good?

- Do you like them?

- Should you switch advisors?

- Do you have an up-to-date succession plan?

- If not do you need one?

Measurable

Investing

- What are the returns on your investments?

- Are these good or poor?

- What do you want?

- Are there risks attached to switching investment classes?

- Do you know exactly what you pay your advisors to manage your investments?

- Are they charging too much?

- Are they good value for money?

- Do you trust them?

Spending

- What are you spending and on what?

- Are you surprised at how much you are spending?

- Do you enjoy your spending?

- Are you getting good value for your money?

- Is it time to make some changes?

Giving

- How much are you giving?

- Who are you giving to?

- What are your reasons for giving and are they still valid?

- Are you surprised at how much you are giving and are you pleased?

- Are you enjoying your giving?

- Should you change the amount and to whom?

Attainable

This is the trickiest aspect of setting goals – you don't know what you do not know. This is where you need to thoroughly explore your goals so you can find out if what you want is actually attainable.

Investing

In the past few decades a lot of research has been done by behavioural scientists on investing behaviour. In setting goals, it should be remembered that the following is typical investor behaviour.

- **Puppy dog enthusiasm.** Once they have made an investment, investors want to convince themselves that they have made the right decision and tend to have puppy dog enthusiasm about the likely outcome and returns from their decision. Some rely on 'gut instinct' which for all but a few seasoned investors means to invest blind. A foolish strategy that is likely to lead to losses.

- **Assumptions based on inadequate knowledge.** Investors think they know more than they actually do. You hear people saying that 'there is nothing better than bricks and mortar', but if you buy a property with a poor tenant's covenant you could be looking at litigation to get the tenant out which could incur considerable legal expenses. Broad generalisations and cliché phrases need watching – therein lies mischief.

- **Following the crowd.** Co-investing is trending – don't get left out, everyone is buying equity – don't miss the boat! If you are being rushed in this manner be careful. Each investment needs a careful review and, if you don't understand what you're doing, don't do it. This is especially true if it is called 'exclusive' or if the referrer is doing you a favour. In both cases proper due diligence is required, because by jumping on the bandwagon without due care and attention, you may lose your funds, and possibly even a friend.

Spending and giving

Puppy dog enthusiasm, assumptions based on inadequate knowledge, following the crowd, and following a friend, apply equally to spending and giving.

In short, most of us, including UHNWs, rarely make decisions based on rational thinking even when we think we are.

In *The Tipping Point* Malcolm Gladwell asserts that decisions are largely controlled by three groups of people; the Mavens who are critical of everything, the Connectors who know everyone, and the Sales People who enthuse others into wanting what everyone else has. The book, a psychological analysis of human decision-making, begins with the premise that logical behaviour does not drive decisions and, therefore, the benefits and what needs to be done must be crystal clear. Then any assumptions need to be tested, tweaked and tested again.

Relevant

This is when you need to look very closely at where you are and where you want to be. Is your goal relevant? You may want to give all your wealth to your children, but if you have no children, it is not relevant!

If you want to treat your wealth seriously, even if your decision is to spend it all before you die, you need to have some idea as to what you like doing and to spend your money accordingly. If you like long walks in the country, and you have a substantial fortune, you are unlikely to spend it before you die, because walking doesn't cost you anything.

Investing

Before investing in art, for example, you may need to learn more about what you like and what makes art valuable. The same goes for any asset class. Handing your wealth to a manager without knowing what he is going to do with your money and what he is investing in on your behalf is to invest blindly.

Spending

What are you spending your money on? George was disappointed after two years of a liquidity event because his lifestyle had not changed. He simply did not know what to spend his money on. He wanted to meet others like him to get some ideas! There is no obligation to spend on cars, holidays or luxuries – it is just that with wealth you can.

Giving

To whom are you giving? Children, grandchildren, or charities? Do you have a succession plan? UHNWs are frequently made to feel guilty about not giving to good causes or preserving their wealth to give to their children. Wealth is like fire: before you give it away, whether to a charity or to your children, make sure that they will make good stewards. There are a lot of charities that do not give as much funding as they could to good causes and a lot of children who would not make good stewards of wealth and could benefit from some training.

Timely

Whatever you want to do make sure you set a time frame to it – things don't get done unless you set a *realistic* time frame. If anyone needs training or education, set a date for when that will happen. Once they've received their training, work out what to do next: make lists and keep to your schedule.

Vision Statement

What are your goals? What is your vision? Write it down as a vision statement.

If you have answered the above questions your vision statement should be clear. It is a natural progression from a dispassionate view of what you are doing already. Without doing the above homework however, it will be difficult to write a vision statement because we are all human and tend to fool ourselves.

> If you are not in control of your wealth your advisors will be and **their goals may not be aligned to yours.**

It is also imperative to put your vision statement and the answers to the preceding questions in writing. This will help you avoid making wrong assumptions based on inadequate knowledge.

If you are serious about making the most of your wealth, you must take some time to learn about it and what you want to do with it. If you are not in control of your wealth your advisors will be and **their goals may not be aligned to yours**.

For more tips and videos please scan the code or copy the link **http://www.garnhamfos.com/wysr-extras/ chapter-1**

In the next section we'll look at advisors' dreams and nightmares. UHNW individuals need to understand them so that they'll be equipped to instruct and monitor their advisors' progress.

Chapter 2
Planning for UHNWs

Chapter summary:

- Is the service you're getting in line with your goals and needs?

- Good and not-so-good ways to choose an advisor.

- The client/advisor relationship.

- Are they serving you – or themselves?

- What to watch out for.

- The internet and comparison websites.

Now you know where you're going, how do you get there?

In Chapter One we looked at where you are and where you want to be. This is such an important first step and not many Ultra High Net Worth individuals do it. But if you don't know where you are and where you want to be, you'll have no idea whether or not you're heading in the right direction.

It has never ceased to amaze me how hard UHNWs work on their businesses and how little attention they seem to give to their wealth once liquid. Tarek had substantial assets held in a Jersey trust. He wanted to take them out of the trust to be managed out of an office in Switzerland. The trust reserved the power to a protector to do this, so there was no difficulty in removing it from Jersey. However, the assets were so poorly documented that it took two years before all the assets and liabilities were known. Only then could we start to effect the transfer. Sadly as soon as the transfer was made Tarek refused to be disciplined with his investments and they soon became muddled again.

If you do not have an up-to-date list of your assets and liabilities, before you go any further **YOU NEED TO GET THIS DONE – NOW**.

Are you allocating enough time to your wealth?

Now that you know what you have and where you are going, you need to allocate some time to understanding who is doing what, the value of what they are doing, and what it is costing.

In the last section we introduced the concept of entropy with regard to wealth. Entropy is the natural tendency for things to deteriorate unless 'energy' is applied. Put simply, if **you** do not know who is doing what, why they are doing it, and how much it is costing, **your wealth will diminish over time**, regardless of who you appoint to look after it.

Appointing an advisor does not mean you can sit back and do nothing. Your advisor will respect what you inspect, and if you don't give your assets a second glance, in time your advisor will come to treat you the same way. As you reflect on the quality of your advisor, think about how engaged you are in the process. If you are not engaged, then you may be criticizing your advisor unfairly.

> If you do not know who is doing what, why they are doing it, and how much it is costing, your wealth will diminish over time.

If you feel you do not understand then take some time to learn, there is lots of information on the internet and there are many courses you can attend.

It's not all about fees

Let's assume you know what you have and what you want to do. You must now review your advisors. Bear in mind that understanding the value of their advice is just as important as knowing what they are doing and how much they are charging.

Here, I am sad to say, most advisors are not very helpful. Of course there are notable exceptions, but most focus on their product or service and how much it costs; not on the benefit or value to you of their service.

My mother was left a substantial portfolio of shares on my grandmother's death which she blindly held onto. At the time of inheriting they were a balanced portfolio, but at the time we looked at it, some 25 years later, half had dropped to zero, a quarter had done moderately well with three or four redeeming stars. In this context the cost of engaging an investment manager merely to reinvest the shares that were on a downward spiral would far outweigh the losses she suffered.

For many the value of investment advice is knowing that someone is looking after your investments and making sensible decisions on a timely basis. The value of this service is being able to sleep at night knowing that someone is looking after your investments for you. However, you need to study the reports when they are delivered and know what is going on.

> For many the value of investment advice is knowing that someone is looking after your investments and making sensible decisions on a timely basis.

Joshua asked me to review his succession arrangements. He could not put his finger on it, but did not like what his local solicitor had drawn up with regard to his will. Joshua was married to Jennifer, his third wife. He had children from both previous wives, but had no children with Jennifer. She had children with a former husband.

The will that had been drawn up for him and Jennifer was to put all the assets of the first to die in a trust for the survivor. The surviving spouse was to act as trustee. The beneficiaries were to be the surviving spouse together with all their children. Joshua was not pleased with the draft he had been given to sign, and decided to get a second opinion before executing it.

Imagine if Joshua had signed this will. On his death, assuming Jennifer survived him, she would be in control of all Joshua's assets as trustee of this will, with the right to appoint everything to herself and her children. Let's assume that she considered Joshua's children to be well provided for by his former wife, and that her children had not been so fortunate. She therefore justifies to herself that it is right and proper to distribute his assets to herself and her children, leaving his children with nothing. Over time, she convinces herself that this is what he would have wanted, because in the letter of wishes it clearly says that she can use her discretion in making distributions.

When I explained this to Joshua, he was horrified. As much as he loved Jennifer and considered her to be fair, he had been divorced twice and was fairly cynical as to the power of love and justice. To his mind wealth and opportunity can distort good intentions. What had been drafted for him was not what he wanted at all.

Once you've found the right advisor, it is important to pay attention to the advice being given. How else will you know whether it is any good or not? You must not leave your

> Don't leave your brain outside your advisor's office.

brain outside your advisor's office. If you don't understand something or something doesn't seem right, ask for clarification. If you continue to be fobbed off or dismissed, or you still cannot understand, then look for another advisor who has more patience or better communication skills.

Most UHNWs choose their advisor haphazardly. I was recently chairing a discussion group of UHNW individuals and quizzed them on how they chose their advisors and their subsequent experiences. Most had chosen their advisors either by a referral from a friend or another advisor, and others found them via the internet. They had then met them on one or more occasions before engaging those they wanted to work with. Every one of the UHNWs had experienced poor and expensive service and they all felt that there was far too much focus on the service and product the advisor was selling rather than on the dreams and nightmares of them, the client.

The client/advisor relationship

- **Your advisor is not a friend**. When you've established a good relationship it may feel that your advisor is the only person who understands what you're trying to do. That is true **because you are paying them**. But if your goals are being influenced by their goals, you may have to sack them.

- **Your advisor is not your slave.** I've seen two types of master-slave relationships and both are problematic. The first is where the client has no concern for the personal circumstances of their advisor. In one situation, Madeline had planned a very special fortieth birthday party for herself; her family and friends were flying in from all over. Chuck, who was a special client of Madeline's, decided to fly in that day and wanted an urgent meeting. Madeline cancelled her birthday party, at some considerable expense – for which Chuck reimbursed her. Madeline's family was furious that Chuck could be so heartless, but he didn't give it a thought.

There is another type of master-advisor relationship that is equally unhelpful. Jonathan had built up a £1 billion business from humble beginnings. He did not suffer fools gladly and was not used to taking advice. Although he instructed Rosalind to prepare a strategy for his philanthropic

> ...if your goals are being influenced by their goals you may have to sack your advisor.

endeavours, he never took the time to listen or read what she wrote, which Rosalind found extremely frustrating. He said she did not understand and what she had learned by assisting others was irrelevant.

Martin is another example. He had a substantial estate, which was in trust. His advisor, Ruth, had told him many times to divide out the family interests from the charitable interests. But he didn't want to take those simple steps before he had the big picture in place. Sadly he died before implementing any changes and the family were at loggerheads with the trustees demanding greater and greater distributions of monies to themselves. If Martin had simply separated out the charitable foundation from the family interests in accordance with what Ruth had recommended he could have ring-fenced monies for the charity, which was now under threat from the ever increasing demands of his children.

- **Your advisor is not your parent.** Don't let them bully you, or bamboozle you with terminology you do not understand. You are the client: you have goals and you have choices and you are **not** an idiot.

Patrick was Karen's advisor. She felt intimidated by the numerous certificates and awards in his office so she accepted what he said about her investments without question – especially as he made it sound so complicated that a mere mortal could not possibly be expected to understand. Karen should have remembered that she was the client and if she didn't understand it was because her advisor was not explaining competently. Of course, there are laws, like tax and cross border succession, that are not easy, logical or straightforward, and laws need to be obeyed. It is not your advisor's fault that the subject of their expertise is complex, however if they fully understand what they are doing they should be able to explain the concepts in a way their clients can understand so that they can make informed decisions.

- **The choice of an advisor is key.** From my experience a poor choice of advisor which leads to a bad experience can usually be tracked down to a failure to set goals and read around the subject, or relying too heavily on personal recommendation and not having read the small print.

It is important to remember that the choice of an advisor will determine the solution. A trust lawyer will give you a trust, a succession lawyer a will and a commercial lawyer a shareholder's agreement – you need to know what you

> ...a poor choice of advisor can usually be tracked down to a failure to set goals and read around the subject...

want. It is similar to recruiting an employee. If you are fuzzy about the job you want doing; the roles, responsibilities and the outcome you're aiming for, you will invariably have a poor relationship from the start which may then be difficult to rectify later.

Referrals from a friend

Be careful. A friend may not know your circumstances, probably does not know your goals and is not a professional who can guide you past the pitfalls. Choosing an advisor is not like choosing which supermarket to go to or which restaurant to eat at. The advisor who might be right for your friend may be totally wrong for you. You must have precise goals and know quite a lot about what you want to achieve when choosing an advisor.

If you decide to take a referral from a friend, you'd need to know how they came to find the advisor, what they used them for and what was the outcome. Most people are reluctant to give this sort of information and so a referral from a friend is likely to be poorly researched. Then there is the personal element. The friend will want to know how you got on, whether you took up their suggestion or not and what was the outcome. You may not want your friend to know that much about your personal circumstances. By all means, go to friends to ask them for a second opinion if they have used an advisor who you are thinking of instructing, but be very cautious if your friend is the only source of recommendation.

Referrals from an advisor

I encourage advisors to have a good professional network; it's an essential part of the culture of care. If they are to care for their clients they need to know their client; the dreams they aspire to and the nightmares they fear. They should not only know who is in their network but what each professional does – in detail.

Richard, an estate agent, had been working closely with Arni and Jezz who were looking to buy an apartment in London. Richard found a spacious flat overlooking Kensington Gardens for them and introduced them to Stephen, who was experienced in conveyancing in the Kensington/Chelsea area.

Then he asked them how long they intended to spend in the UK every year. He said they should know the tax rules and introduced them to Nick, a tax accountant. He also said they needed to understand the immigration rules so he shared an article written by Rosemary, an immigration expert. Then he asked if they needed an interior designer and gave them a book written by Jane. Jezz liked Jane's style. Finally Richard said that if they wanted to get make new friends in London they could join an investment club of like-minded people who would be able to find them schools for their children, good restaurants and shops.

If Richard wanted to develop the relationship with Arni and Jezz further and make sure they continued to think of him, he could arrange a brief catch-up the following month to ask how they were getting on. Arni and Jezz could be a good source of referrals for him. He could also catch up with Stephen, Nick, Rosemary and Jane to see how they were getting on with the couple. They may also have clients looking to move and he wants them to recommend him.

A referral from an advisor is good news – especially if they are well read as to the value of their service to their clients.

Having extolled the virtues of taking referrals from a professional, don't engage any advisor blindly. If you don't understand something. or it looks too good to be true, or you feel you are just following the herd, take a moment to think it through. People have been caught out in Ponzi schemes, they've been sold, mis-sold and bribed.

Remember Madoff?

Madoff was 70 when he went to prison. He was widely considered to have the magic touch as an investor, but in reality he had created a massive Ponzi scheme which he packaged as a hedge fund called Ascot. Ponzi schemes pay out returns on the capital invested by others, so as long as the money remains invested and more people join it can continue. Investors across the New York area clamoured to be in Ascot; it was 'too good to be true' with consistent double-digit returns. The Ascot investments were being recommended by reputable investment managers, who were finding it difficult to match. It was also exclusive – you could only get in through a referral from the right people.

If Madoff hadn't faced $7 billion in redemptions at the turn of the recession, this Ponzi scheme might not have been discovered.

Many have expressed astonishment as to how he got away with it for so long. But if you look at it in the context of human behaviour, the analysis of trust and the exclusive nature of the investment, it is not that surprising. As we will explore in part four, humans follow others, especially if they are seen to be people of influence.

Inducements and commissions

It is not only referrals from advisors where caution is needed; it is also the products recommended by an advisor from a third party, such as an insurer or an investment promoter.

> People have been caught out in Ponzi schemes, sold, mis-sold and bribed.

43

Ashley was a client of Benjamin, a private banker. He inherited a small sum of money from a maiden aunt in Scotland and asked Benjamin whether he had any ideas. Benjamin suggested an offshore insurance package that would provide him with tax free income for twenty years. Did he want to take it or not? At this point Ashley should have asked himself what Benjamin would be making out of this recommendation.

In January 2013, the Financial Conduct Authority (FCA) banned the practice of insurers and wealth management firms providing financial incentives and commission structures to advisors who promoted their products. The concern was that in providing an incentive the financial advisor would be tempted to 'push' the product with the highest payment rather than the one that best served the client's interests.

Later that year, the FCA investigated the practices of 26 life insurers and advisors to provide information about their service or distribution agreements; in total it received and reviewed 80 agreements. The regulator said that just over half the firms it sampled had agreements in place that it considered to breach its inducement rules and the objectives of their retail distribution review (RDR).

It also identified concerns over certain types of joint ventures between providers and advisors that were not consistent with the objectives of the RDR. The FCA's findings included:

- Some payments by life insurers to advisors appeared to be linked to securing sales of their products; this included an increase in spending on support services (such as research or management information) provided by advice firms in the lead up to, and after, the implementation of the new advice rules. In many cases the FCA did not think the business benefit of these increases was justified nor did it improve the quality of service to the customer.

- There were financial arrangements in place with life insurers that incentivised advisors to promote a specific provider's product to their clients, creating a risk that advice would be influenced more by commercial decisions than the interests of their clients.

- Further, the FCA also identified that certain joint ventures, where a new investment proposition was jointly designed by providers and advisors, could create conflicts of interest and potentially lead to biased advice. In one example, the advisor was paid substantial up-front fees by the provider with its profits increasing the more it channelled business into the joint venture.

The FCA's review found some life insurance firms had arrangements in place that could influence advisors. This ran counter to the RDR's aim of removing commission bias. The FCA has since reported that many of the firms involved in the review have now changed their arrangements. This means that Ashley is now less likely to be sold an investment because of the advantages to Benjamin rather than the benefit to himself.

> The FCA's review found some life insurance firms had arrangements in place that could influence advisors.

Ashley should however, remain cautious. These arrangements are almost impossible for the client to identify or to elicit bias by asking questions of his advisor. If the advisor is feathering his own nest in selling the product he is hardly going to admit to it! Clients need to rely on the FCA to have a sufficiently robust deterrent in place to stamp out such poor practices.

Mis-selling

Another concern is mis-selling. This is where an advisor's employees are incentivised to push the products that earn the most profit for their employer. As you can see from the previous chapter, advisors are encouraged to identify the work and clients that make them the most profit. If they are encouraged to 'push products' that are not in the best interests of their client, or even totally out of alignment with what the client is trying to achieve, then that is mis-selling and the Financial Conduct Authority can fine the offender.

With inducements Ashley from the above example needs to be concerned about the commission the insurance company that provides the product is paying Benjamin, with mis-selling Ashley needs to be concerned about how much Benjamin's employer is paying him for recommending one investment over another.

The government has long been concerned about the vulnerability of people seeking advice from professionals, and the area in which there has been the most criticism has been with the insurers and wealth advisors.

With a few notable exceptions many private banks have been fined by the FCA for mis-selling – whether it is unnecessary products to the elderly or to other vulnerable parties who do not understand what it is they are buying.

> Many private banks have been fined by the FCA for mis-selling...

Mis-selling is the antithesis of trust. Trust is looking after the best interest of clients, mis-selling blatantly ignores the interests of the client to drive up profits for the advisor. The advisor is seen to be a person of influence and the FCA does not want advisors to use their influence to sell products that are not in the best interests of the client. It is these bad practices that have given these institutions a poor reputation.

Bribery

The Bribery Act 2010 is another example where the Government has stepped in to protect the vulnerable and weak.

It is now illegal to pay or receive a bribe. An offence will be committed if Andrew, who is an advisor to Brian, offers Brian a financial or other advantage to encourage him to buy services and products that he may not otherwise be interested in. As a professional advisor Andrew needs to act impartially and in Brian's best interests at all times.

Geoffrey is a private banker. Every year he would give his best clients a Christmas gift. One year he gave his favourite client a safari hat, his preferred cigars and a tie he'd said he liked. Following the Bribery

Act, Geoffrey has now been told to stop making these gifts, much to annoyance of his client. However, the client has not taken his business elsewhere. So it is arguable that the gift was not a bribe and was merely part of the Geoffrey's culture of care for his clients.

How does this affect corporate hospitality? It is one thing to give small gifts to a loyal customer, but what about gifts to induce them to become a client – such as the typical and enjoyable corporate hospitality? The statutory guidance suggests that corporate hospitality does not amount to a bribe provided that the hospitality has a legitimate business aim (including developing relationships), is reasonable, proportionate and appropriate in the circumstances (with reference to what is normal in the particular industry).

What to watch out for

Wealth advisors and insurers are running a business, which means they have to make a profit for their shareholders or partners. Given that the FCA has stamped on practices such as commissions and bribery, and is generally promoting transparency and openness with fees and charges, you should consider the following before engaging an advisor who is selling you a product or providing you with a service.

- **The more layers in the product between you and the investment the more it is costing you in fees.** If a product involves insurance, an offshore special purpose vehicle or whatever, each layer will need to be paid for, and it is not always easy to find out how much.

- **The more components there are to a structure, the more it will cost you in fees** – whether it be a trust, offshore company or special purpose vehicle. Make sure they are there for a purpose and know what that purpose is, before committing to it.

- **Tax is extremely complex and there are literally hundreds of pages of anti-avoidance legislation**. If the extra layers are there to avoid tax tread with extreme caution. The government in every country is on red alert to stamp out tax avoidance and will do whatever it can to stop it.

- **The fewer intermediaries** there are between you and the investment manager the fewer the people you have to pay.

- **If your advisor is charging for his or her time**, spend more time doing your homework and cut the amount you have to pay them. If you know what assets you have, have set your goals and done your homework, you are in the driving seat in managing your wealth and instructing the right people to assist you. We are living in a digital revolution, the information is readily available.

If your advisors do not give you the information you need in a format you can understand, such as case studies and testimonials, find others that do. You can always switch advisors. Comparison websites and platforms are springing up all the time – the UHNW individual is not stupid, they learn fast – and they are no longer prepared to accept sweet talking or to be bamboozled by jargon.

The internet and comparison websites

Henrik, a member of one of the best known and richest families in the world, was looking for a public relations advisor. Rather than ask a friend or an advisor, he decided to do his research online. When asked why, Henrik said he did not want to be influenced by anyone and did not want anyone knowing too much about his private life.

With the onslaught of the digital age, personal information can be in the public domain within minutes. Well-known families value their privacy and are rightly concerned about their confidentiality. Increasingly they take the view that the less people know about their private matters the better. The expression 'the walls have ears' has never been more true than now.

It is certainly the case that most professionals take care to maintain their clients' privacy, but when it comes to making recommendations and referrals an increasing number of UHNW individuals prefer that the fewer people who know about their issues the better. They are looking to find their own advisors through the internet and comparison websites.

All too frequently, I hear advisors saying that UHNWs would not use comparison websites or the internet to find an advisor. This is simply not true. Scorpio, the consultant to UHNW individuals and their advisors, has revealed that the UHNW community is three times more likely to use comparison websites than anyone else.

The UHNW community needs to wake up to the fact that they don't have to put up with poor service. Advice they should demand from their advisor needs to be compelling and client-focused. They need their advisors to tell them why their services and products make a difference to them; what value do they provide and why.

> The UHNW community is three times more likely to use comparison websites than anyone else.

How to avoid bad experiences

To avoid bad experiences you need to know what you have, how much it is costing, and where you want to go. Your questions need to be answered so that you understand what you need to do and why. Then, when you have done your homework, fix up an introduction or meeting and make a list of the questions you want to ask.

Probably the most relevant question to ask an advisor is whether they have clients like you. What did they do for them, what was the outcome and what did it cost? Do they offer events or education-based training? Clients love to meet other clients and wealth advisors do too little to promote those opportunities. Satisfied clients are an advisor's best ambassadors and one of the greatest ways to cross-sell their services at next to no cost. If the advisor does host such an event you can ask to meet existing clients and then you can see for yourself whether this advisor is right for you.

For more tips and videos please scan the code or copy the link **http://www.garnhamfos.com/wysr-extras/ chapter-2**

The next section deals with how you manage your time, are you a busy fool, minute wise, but hour foolish? – None of us can turn back the clock – so we need to view our time and how we spend it as one of our most valuable commodities.

Chapter 3
Time management for UHNWs

Chapter summary:

- Are you busy – or productive?

- Make a list and manage your time.

- Is travel *really* necessary?

- The benefits of online networking.

- 'Busy fools' put their lives and wellbeing on the line.

Time unites everyone, but do we use it wisely?

Wasting time is to my mind a sin. I am not talking about spending time pleasurably or taking time to reflect or meditate – these pursuits are not a waste of time. Time is very much like wealth; once it is gone, it is gone. You cannot get it back. Just as some people squander money, many of us are guilty of squandering time.

If we are serious about making and smashing our goals we need to be serious about not wasting time. All humans are the same, whether UHNW individuals or advisors, so in this section I haven't made any distinction between the two communities.

I want to go through my eight steps of how time is thrown away to enable us to focus on making the best use of it so we can attain and exceed our goals.

Proactive not reactive: do you have a minute?

I have had the honour of working with some hugely successful individuals who are, almost without exception, generous with their time – because they are proactive and not reactive.

Is this you?

You get to your desk to find 40 unopened emails and two letters. You start on the emails and the first requires you to open a folder and refresh yourself on some details, but you haven't got time for that. You move on to the next, the phone rings, a colleague wants to drop in for a chat, he is concerned about a sensitive issue, you look at the calendar and make a time to meet. You go back to your emails and delete a few, then your assistant comes in.

> Lack of time management is not only detrimental to your health... it is also stopping you from achieving your goals.

"Do you have a minute?" You like to keep an open door policy, so you chat to your assistant until the telephone rings; your assistant waits while you take the call, and then your secretary comes in with some magazines and post, you glance through the magazines and a press release about a client catches your eye, you add it to the pile on your desk that you fully intend to read later.

If this sounds familiar you are working in a reactive and not a proactive manner, your business is running you – and you are not running your business.

You are allowing people to interrupt your life with "do you have a minute" meetings, telephone calls and emails that disturb you all day long, leaving you with only your free time to plan and do what you need to do to make and smash your goals. This lack of time management is not only detrimental to your health and home life; it is also stopping you from achieving your goals.

Time managers and time wasters

I was always amazed at how calm my UHNW clients are. I came to the conclusion that these captains of industry were more disciplined and organised with their time than most advisors.

Firstly, if someone said 'have you got a minute' the answer would be "No. Book a time in the diary and come prepared with an agenda, considered questions and a suggestion about the solution." In this way, both sides were prepared to consider the issue, quietly and without interruptions, and the result was usually much more worthwhile.

The second great interrupter is the telephone. If you don't have a secretary and you've allocated time to a meeting or working on a project, set a voicemail that says you're working and will call back later, with a request to know what the call was concerning. Nine times out of ten a call is not worth taking, because it could either have been dealt with by someone else, or the matter has passed.

Emails are a third source of distraction and interruption. Once again it's not necessary to deal with these immediately, do what you've planned to do and then make time to work through all of them. Some of you may laugh – I have a poor reputation for answering emails, because for a long time I did not allocate time to dealing with them. The same principle applies to LinkedIn, Twitter, Instagram and other social media platforms.

One word of warning to the 'I am so busy' junky. If you start becoming proactive and stop being reactive, it will feel like you are not very busy. This is not a comfortable feeling for those who measure their importance by how much they are in demand. Once again it comes down to what you are trying to achieve, are you trying to make and smash your goals? Then you need to free up more time to do so.

> It's not about how busy you are – it's about how productive you are.

Are you fooling yourself into thinking that 'no-one could be working harder at making their goals happen'? It's not about how busy you are – it's about how *productive* you are. If you're being productive, you really need to be more disciplined and focused on running your business rather than letting it run you.

Touch it once and list making

I am fortunate to have been a Trustee of the Household Cavalry Museum which is in the corner of the Parade Ground just off St James's Park, backing onto Whitehall. The Household Cavalry are the soldiers on the black horses that guard the official entrance to Buckingham Palace off Whitehall and have those amazing fountain-like plumes cascading from their helmets.

One of the time management lessons taught in the army is to touch something only once; decide then and there what you are going to do with what you have touched and when. Put it on your list and in your diary. With regard to emails, make some files called Prepare, Action, Reading and Waiting. When you read them make sure you filter according to author or subject so that you deal with all aspects relating to that project together. This saves a huge amount of time and ensures you don't miss important relevant messages.

Be absolutely insistent that everyone puts the same subject heading in the subject line, so important messages don't slip or get overlooked. Also insist that emails cover one issue only so that they can be read with others on that issue and can be filed appropriately as well. Ban emails that deal with a range of issues, they will waste your time and could lead to important information slipping through the net. If you can't leave an email unanswered, turn off the alert button. Make sure you are in control of your emails: do not let them control you.

Make sure that every time you touch something and cannot deal with it then and there that it is filed in a pending file, **and** included in a list.

Now you need to manage your list. You need to make an A list and a B list. Ask yourself: "What are the eight most important things to do today that will help me achieve my goals?" This is your A list. You should never have more than eight things on your A list because it will overwhelm you and the big, important things that need to be done to make and smash your goals simply won't get done.

As you cross things off your A list, you will need to add to it from your B list. Personally, I prefer not to revise my lists as I cross each one off. It is psychologically good to see the list diminish during the day. I prune and rearrange the lists on a daily basis according to priorities, but it is these lists that keep my time management under control.

> What are the eight most important things I need to do today that will help me achieve my goals?

I also include in these lists a number of personal items, which otherwise I would just not get done, in my enthusiasm to tick items off my list.

1. List management: prioritise and plan

As you prepare your lists allocate time and a priority level to them. Let's say an invoice query comes in. You decide it will take half an hour, but it needs to be done urgently because it is important to you to manage clients and their expectations. You put this task into your A list and a less pressing matter you move down to your B list to do when you have a little more time.

Another trick is to do the hardest things that take the longest time in the morning and save the more pleasurable or shorter things for the afternoon, when you are feeling a little more tired.

I was involved in litigation which went on for several years – the email threads were incredible – everyone was copied in to everything and felt it their duty to say something about everything. And so the bills kept going out and nothing got done. I was involved in another litigation that also went on for many years, but in this case the project was planned – who would receive what and report to whom. Although considerable time was spent in planning the project, years and millions of pounds were saved by planning how to handle things right at the start. You may say that planning saw the lawyers lose years of fees. That's true, but having seen the time wasted on the first project, I would emphatically not recommend that firm to another client or use them myself, while I certainly would with the second. Time management should be one of the crucial questions asked of an advisor who is billing on time, but from my experience no one ever asked me that question.

> Time management should be one of the crucial questions asked of an advisor who is billing on time...

While on the subject of litigation, I have always taken the view that it should be the last resort because it is costly and time consuming. I've always favoured mediation. However, in light of recent experience, I would now say that it depends. If either side is totally intransigent or there is unlikely to be any movement, which is often the case with family disputes, sometimes going to court where a judge can make an order that is enforceable is the best and most cost-effective route. The earlier you take that route the better so as not to allow entrenched positions to develop.

If a project is likely to take a long time, such as a report, drafting a contract or reading a detailed letter, you need to break it down into manageable chunks and allocate time over a period to get it done. I love large projects, but there are many people who put them off because they see it as a massive task. It is like the children's joke 'How do you eat an elephant? One bite at a time.'

As you look at your A list, put 'to do' tasks in your diary and stick to those times and dates. It chunks up your day and makes you feel in control. It also stops any temptation to allow the 'do you have a minute' meetings to creep back because your diary clearly tells you that you do not. You have allocated your time to something that needs doing now, so book a time when the 'just a minute' query can be dealt with according to priority. Make sure you allocate the requisite amount of time needed to deal with it.

If you are running a business, you need to make sure that not only you, but all your team are making lists, prioritising and planning their day. A small but focused team always outperforms larger and disorganised teams.

2. List management: short communications and clean desks

If you are making lists and prioritising your day, you should not have anything on your desk and all your communications should be brief.

I found a clean desk policy one of the hardest things to implement. Having a busy desk made me feel busy, but in fact most of what was on my desk was clutter that I never looked at. Furthermore, when I did make an attempt to tame my feral desk, I was often surprised by what was on it. When I tried to find something it always took a long time, whereas if I had filed it when I had it in my hand, or thrown it away knowing that I had an electronic version in a file on my server, I'd have saved myself a lot of time and headaches.

> If you are making lists and prioritising your day, you should not have anything on your desk...

An extremely successful client of mine would physically tear up old drafts if they had been superseded. If you are doing things electronically then you must make sure you date the draft and number it, so you always know which one is current.

It is well understood that 80% of filed information is never looked at again. So ask yourself: "if I need this in future could I find it again from some other source?" I do a lot of writing and some ideas and articles trigger thoughts, so I put these into my reading file, most things I store electronically and do not print out at all. As my desk became clearer, the better I got at managing my electronic filing system. I learned to file as I went along, but only if I needed the document later.

My UHNW community tends to write short messages such as 'Yes'. If you top and tail every email with pleasantries think of how many hours you must be wasting. Don't get me wrong, pleasantries are necessary for your best clients and the key people who help you achieve your goals, but they are just not needed for everyone all the time.

The other thing to watch is the time you take for a meeting. I used to work at Simmons & Simmons with Edward Troup, who subsequently became very senior in HM Treasury. He queried why meetings needed to last a whole hour. Most meetings can be over and done in much less time – but somehow they drag and drivel on until the full hour is up.

Provided it is made clear that the meeting will be short, "I think we can get through all we need within twenty minutes", and you have circulated this note before the meeting, then no one will be offended.

3. List management: do you have time for a coffee?

As a lawyer, before I adopted a very disciplined approach to winning business, I was astonished at how much time could be spent in having coffee. If each meeting lasted an hour, it can take hours and hours out of your day. When I first worked as a lawyer it seemed that everyone was making time for coffee with anyone who suggested it. It seemed that this was what advisors did to win new business, but I couldn't understand why. When I took over as head of the group at Simmons & Simmons I simply did not have the time for everyone who wanted to have coffee if I wanted to run the group and look after my clients. I needed to set goals and meet only those people who could be useful in getting me where I needed to go, otherwise it was a waste of time.

> Provided it is made clear that the meeting will be short... no one will be offended.

Once you have set your goals and you know who you want to target, may I suggest that you go back over your diary for the previous year and add up the time spent in meetings with people who are no longer on your list. How much time did you waste? Did these people ever refer any work to you?

Then it's a good idea to go over what you do before and after a meeting. How many meetings do you go to where you put the meeting in your diary but do not do any research on the person you are going to meet beforehand? Is there anything about them on LinkedIn? What does Google have on them? Is there anything on BConnect Club? Do they have a Twitter page? What is said about them on their website and in their brochure? After you've done your homework, you need to know what it is you want to achieve in some detail and make sure it is aligned to your goals – if not the meeting will be a waste of time.

One of my most high profile clients had appointed a prominent gatekeeper to assist her in sorting out a few personal issues in a discreet and private manner. He invited me for a coffee. I knew that if we got on personally I would remain appointed but if we didn't, I could lose the mandate.

It soon became obvious from my research that Michael, my client's gatekeeper, was keen on country sports, so one of my goals for the meeting was to steer the conversation to country sports, which was one of my hobbies at the time. It was very easy to engage him on his favourite pastime and it was easy thereafter to turn the subject to what he needed to do to assist his client. I easily won the business.

On another occasion, I had been doing some very low grade work for Roger, a whopper of a client, who I had not met in person. First I got to know his right-hand man and discussed some concerns before making a few suggestions as to how they could be resolved.

Roger was coming to London and, through his right-hand man, he agreed to have a coffee. I was warned that I'd probably get about ten minutes, if that, and had to get my message across effectively because I wouldn't have a second chance. I didn't have an opportunity to speak at the meeting because some other advisors were there too. As the ten minutes drew to a close, Roger turned to me and asked for my opinion on the issues. I had less than ten seconds. I had prepared what I was going say so delivered it in less than 10 seconds. He smiled and told me I had the business.

On another occasion, I had a two hour preliminary meeting with advisors. After the meeting, Don, one of the advisors, telephoned us and said that our client, who was a very distinguished woman, was coming to London and wanted to meet for a coffee. He confided that she had a keen eye for fashion and would expect us to have the right type of handbags.

I went to the partnership to ask them for a 'firm's bag budget' which was based on the money we would have had to spend on flying to meet her, hotel accommodation and time out of the office. We arrived at the meeting and the three ladies in the team plonked their new handbags on the table. We won the business.

4. List management: travel – is it essential?

Travelling is such a waste of time. You need to ask yourself the question – why? Of course you must travel to see clients, not all of them want or can come to see you. Most of the time, the clients will pay for your expenses, but not always for your time. When you factor in the time; travelling to the airport, waiting for the

> The focus is: think smarter, not harder.

plane to take off, flying, landing and getting to where you need to go, let alone the time when you are there, catching up on sleep, meetings and eating – is it worth it?

If it will help you achieve your goals then every moment is time well-spent, but what about business development trips? I have seen colleagues spend hours and hours travelling abroad to see a list of contacts that have neither been qualified nor pre-screened. As a result they get a lot of small ticket work and instructions from intermediaries, without working for the client direct.

The focus is think smarter, not harder.

About fifteen or so years ago we wanted to develop business relations in Switzerland, so we hired a decent venue and invited those we wanted to see to a small, intimate event. We made sure that we had done our homework on every single one of the attendees, especially on what would interest them. Then we needed to make sure that what we did was clearly communicated to our chosen audience.

My preference was to give a talk liberally peppered with case studies so that what I did was clearly conveyed in the message. Everyone loves stories – and it is the easiest and most effective way to convey a message. Other advisors used role playing which was also very effective.

However, is there now any need to travel? Would it not be just as effective to arrange for the seminar or role play to be videoed and invite your audience to view it online? You can follow up by asking them whether your expertise is of any relevance to their clients, if they come back by saying yes – **then** follow up with a visit if appropriate. When you meet them you can reciprocate by asking what they do that could be of interest to your clients – in this way you are building the basis of a reciprocal trusted relationship.

There are other things you can do remotely. If one of your key contacts resides abroad you do not have to meet them to keep in touch, in fact your connections could be more meaningful if you don't just rely on face-to-face contact. Let's say that you think Charlie has the sort of clients you'd also like as clients and is in a position to refer them to you for the work you are good at.

If you do your homework you may discover that he's speaking at a conference in Miami. Rather than go to Miami you could write to Charlie to say you've noticed that he's speaking, you're sorry you won't be there, but could he possibly send you his notes? If he does, read them and make comments. Make a point of saying that you have clients for which the work he does may be of interest. If he responds you can tell him what you are doing for those clients and ask whether he has clients for which your services may be of use. If he doesn't have any such clients, move on, Charlie is a waste of time. However, if he says that his clients do need the services you provide from time to time, give him your full culture of care treatment. Follow what he does and make a point of continuing the dialogue, add him to your Google alerts, comment on his posts and the people with whom he is connected in LinkedIn; you have saved time and expense by not travelling and are on the way to winning new business, all from the comfort of your own office.

5. List management: networking

Everyone needs to network to win new business, some do it well and others do not. Let's take a typical networking scenario, such as a seminar or conference. You spend the time listening to speeches and then over coffee, lunch or tea, make as many connections and collect as many cards as you can. You follow up or not, as the case may be.

> You need to pick the seminars or events that will put you in touch with people who are going to help you meet your goals.

From your goal setting you will know what clients you're looking for and for what type of work. You need to pick the seminars or events that will put you in touch with people who are going to help you meet your goals.

Maybe you need to keep up to date, to learn or gain CPD points. This must be viewed separately from networking. At these types of seminars you are likely to meet people like you with whom you may have interesting conversations, but you are unlikely to win new business because you are among your competitors.

Attending seminars to gain CPD points may no longer be the most cost effective or time efficient way of learning. A far easier way to learn is online through videos, training modules and webinars.

Networking should be very focused, if the people you are meeting at an event are not in a position to assist you in winning your goals don't go, what is the point? Of course, if you enjoy meeting people who won't assist you in getting to your goals then recognise it for what it is – a social occasion. Don't kid yourself that in some fashion it will win you new business. If the people you are meeting do not have the sort of clients you are looking for and cannot refer you the type of work you want, no matter how well you get on you will simply not get any referral business.

The same is true of any other form of networking such as Twitter, Facebook or LinkedIn. If you are connected to people who are not in a position to help you meet your goals then what is the point in being connected and spending time connecting? Of course, it gives a nice warm feeling to know you have thousands of followers, but they need to be the right type and you only know this if you are certain of your goals and what you want to achieve.

> Online networking is far more efficient than offline networking.

Network online as well, which is far more effective and efficient than offline networking. Follow those you think have clients that could be your ideal clients. Make sure they can see you and you can see them. Keep in touch and show an interest, it is far more effective than being in the same room and collecting a card.

Your time is precious

All work and no play is not a good balance. It is absolutely essential to factor in some 'you' time. If you are disciplined and focused and use the tips and tactics outlined above, you will have plenty of time not only for you, but also for your key clients when you are not charging them. You need to work out how best to use this time and this can be just as much a challenge as learning how to meet and smash your targets, whether it be with your wealth or working for people with wealth.

Many of the UHNW individuals I have worked with who are very focused on time management are also very clued up as to how to spend their spare time. Pierre would go fishing and I don't mean trout fishing, I mean deep sea fishing. He was brought up on and by the sea, so it was not a passion that he developed in his later years, it had been a passion since childhood. Of course the fishing boat, which had a fighting chair in the middle surrounded by twelve rods and was managed by a gilly, was not large enough for him and his family and friends to sleep and relax, so he would moor it alongside his yacht, where he ate and slept. I was standing next to him on the yacht when his fishing boat came in sight. "Look at that Caroline," he said. "What a beauty."

Another very wealthy man, Adrian, was not so keen on fishing as Pierrre, but liked his sailing. He also liked his comforts and his sleek sailing boat, for which he needed a crew of 12, was just too small to sleep and dine comfortably so he had what he called his 'kitchen' boat. This ocean going yacht would go on ahead to a chosen destination so that by the time he and his crew had raced there they could relax on the 'kitchen' boat and have a good meal without having to wait or go ashore. In both cases, and I could cite many more, the attention to detail and the planning was impressive.

For some it has taken time to find out how they want to spend their spare time. As I said previously, the first five years following a liquidity event are the most vulnerable, and when coupled with the 'mortgages to management' anxiety, can be dangerous. It is often overlooked how many celebrities turn to drugs or drink to deal with this anxiety during this time; they are literally 'killing' time, but if not careful could also succeed in killing themselves. This is when they need loved ones to understand what it is they are going through, or coaching and assistance so they can find their feet and a platform for their money.

Many advisors I have worked with have an unhealthy work/life balance. Male advisors have a tendency towards being busy fools, answering all the emails as they come in, and leaving meetings and mealtimes to answer calls. It was particularly prevalent in the company commercial departments when I started out my legal profession.

You would get a roomful of anything up to 20 advisors working to close a deal, all with their jackets off and many wearing braces. At about 10 p.m. they would send out for some food such as pizzas, which they'd eat, usually standing up. Hours would be wasted as they waited for the documents to be amended and points finalised. They were all very earnest and serious, but a lot of it was a waste of time. The following day, they would be eager to tell their colleagues in hushed tones that it was 'an all nighter'. Very often they would abandon dinner parties, theatre tickets and holidays to engage in sessions with the increasing risk of health problems, little time spent with the children and possibly even divorce.

> Are you are a 'busy fool' who has let work take control of your life? Then you are at risk.

There are a lot of self help books on how to get back in touch with life, so I only want to make a few personal observations here. Are you a 'busy fool' who has let work control your life? Then you are at risk. If for whatever reason work stops, whether on retirement, or redundancy, a take-over, or a downturn in the market, you are in danger. If you don't have strong family bonds you won't have support when you need it and you are likely to feel useless and a failure.

Simon was an extremely successful advisor who decided to take early retirement to focus for a year on a book he was writing. He confided in me after three months, saying that he felt a failure and a lack of respect. This was a man who was often called 'brilliant' by his peers. I assured him

> 'Oblivion drinking' is on the increase among women advisors – especially amongst those who are juggling a family as well as a career.

he was not a failure, it just felt like that because he wasn't as busy or in demand. It wasn't long before his book was finished, his brilliance more widely recognised and he was back in demand – possibly more so than before.

There is one danger that is on the increase for many women advisors – especially amongst those women juggling a family as well as a career – the tendency towards 'oblivion drinking'.

As they come home from a stressful day, and before they bathe the kids and prepare a meal for the family, they have a glass of wine, 'to help me wind down'. And after the family chores and evening meal another glass or two follows to 'help me sleep'. The wine does not really aid sleep as it interferes with rapid eye movement, which is the deep cycle of sleep that aids memory and restores the body, and so the next day the body's ability to function is impaired. Weight is not lost, complexions are dulled and the woman feels more and more anxious – which leads to a further need for a drink.

There are personality types of women prone to this type of behaviour, the Pleasers, the Perfectionist, the Inner Critic and the Inner Child. I have come across many advisors who like to please their clients who are the last to leave the bar at conferences pleasing everyone but themselves.

One of the most balancing and rewarding things I do is meditating every morning for half an hour. If normal life is like a child's snow dome, with the snow blurring the scene, then meditating is what happens when you stop shaking the dome. The snow starts to settle and things become clearer. I also walk in the park every day and this walk brings clarity and joy, which makes me feel good for the rest of the day. I have no idea whether my meditation is correct. I went to Asia to find out, but my guide said it was better not to interfere; it was working for me so he let me get on with it.

I also do some yoga, not for any other reason than I am getting older and need to remain supple, I also swim and like to cook and eat, but on the whole prefer a life full of simple pleasures.

For more tips and videos please scan the code or copy the link **http://www.garnhamfos.com/wysr-extras/ chapter-3**

Next we turn to Getting There once we know what we want, planned how to get there and observed how we spend our time – we need to Get there.

Chapter 4
Getting there: UHNWs

Chapter summary:

- What to look for in an advisor.

- The advisor audit.

- Building your inner circle of advisors.

- Forming a family office.

- Does your advisor share your values and interests?

Knowing yourself: getting started

Now you have set your goals, had a critical look at where you are and what you do with your time, you need to take the reins and get there. UHNWs have the same difficulty in taking control of advice and advisors as pupils do with their tutors. How do you take control when the person you are paying has more knowledge than you? A pupil has to trust his tutor knows the syllabus, that she knows the subject and is telling him what he needs to know. Taking advice is like being a pupil; you are in a position of vulnerability. So you need to do some homework before committing yourself to someone who has the power of knowledge over you.

What to look for in an advisor

1. Qualifications.

- What qualifications does your advisor have and has anyone checked them?
- Ask for their curriculum vitae and check it for oddities in their professional career.
- Take references.

2. Track record.

- Ask for case studies, what have they done for other clients?
- Testimonials: what do their clients say about them?
- Who do they network with and do they recommend them?
- What are their values and interests?
- How well do they communicate with their network?

3. Do you feel you could trust them?

- Are they interested in finding out your goals and assisting you in meeting them?
- Are they dominating the conversation with their jargon and projections?
- Have they listened to you or do they blindly interpret what you are saying according to their own goals?
- Are they transparent, honest and clear in what they are communicating, or do you feel bamboozled?
- Are they focused on you rather than on them?

4. How financially secure are they?

Once upon a time you would never dream of asking whether a bank or law firm was financially secure but it cannot be ignored now, especially if the bank or law firm is going to hold your money.

- What is their professional insurance cover like?
- How robust is their internal governance? Could a rogue dealer hold the organization and your money to ransom?

- Are they at risk from natural disasters? The Cayman Islands, for example, is in danger of flooding and the Bahamas to hurricanes. Do they have offsite disaster recovery?
- What is the system of checks and standards?
- Do they have enough resources to keep going if a major client leaves, or to cover their new office expansion?
- Have they invested in technology and training to ensure the staff remains up-to-date and efficient?
- What do they do internally and what do they outsource?
- What is the ownership of the organization?
- Which regulatory body do they report to?
- Have there been any irregularities or warnings?
- Are there any conflicts of interest you should know about?
- Does the wealth advisor pay commission to third parties or receive any commission from third parties?
- What are the policies and procedures to protect client confidentiality?
- Have there been any leaks to the press?
- Have there been criminal investigations of any member of staff or another such enquiry, and how was it dealt with?
- Have they engaged in a voluntary financial arrangement?

5. How do they pay themselves?

Although I'll deal with this in greater detail in part six, suffice it to say that now you need to know how they charge you and how they reward themselves. This can be the key factor in whether you get a good or mediocre service.

Is it time to switch advisors? It is not for me to say when you should switch advisors, but remember you are the client and it is your goals that your advisor should be helping you meet, not theirs.

Are your advisors delivering what you want?

How well do you know your advisors? I don't mean whether you know they support Chelsea, have three daughters and enjoy choral music, here I am talking about their terms and conditions, their performance, their reports and what they have billed you so far and for what.

If you don't know you need to:

- Know their terms and conditions.

- Look at their performance.

- Look and their reports.

- Look at their bills.

- Look at their engagement letter.

- Look at what they say on their website.

- Find out what you can about them personally on Google, LinkedIn, Twitter and elsewhere, and;

- Is it a consistent message or are you utterly confused?

Remember, you are the client and you are paying a fee for their service so you need to understand the value and benefit of what you are buying and if it's worth the amount you are being charged. If you don't know, you need to ask or find out.

Choosing an advisor

If you have done your homework well, you should by now have a good picture of :

- Where you are.

- Where you want to be.

- Where the shortfalls are in terms of your existing advisors, and;

- Where are the gaps?

You now need to set about choosing an advisor. The following steps are just as relevant to evaluating your existing advisors as they are to choosing a new one. The digital age has led to an explosion of information so it should be easy to get started. The only difficulty is that if you do not know what the outcome is going to look like it's not always easy to know what you need to search for.

In search of a general practitioner

I have long been concerned that for a UHNW individual there are few if any general practitioners who can set them off in the right direction. If I have a back ache I'll go to my doctor who may suggest I go to an osteopath. If there were no doctor, I would need to choose which specialist to go to myself. If I went to an osteopath I would get manipulated, a personal trainer, exercise; an acupuncturist, needles; a surgeon, an operation and so on – who I go to determines the outcome.

Fifty years ago, a UHNW individual would go to his local solicitor for general advice, but now all solicitors are specialists. Private banks evolved to step into this role. Unlike most solicitors, they are commercial; evaluate a need, look for a solution, develop a product to meet it and then sell it.

> Professionals needn't work in silos. To embrace the culture of care, they need to be part of the client's 'Ring of Confidence'.

Before FATCA was introduced in the US, a withholding tax was implemented, private banks in particular in Switzerland such as Credit Suisse advised their clients to set up companies in the British Virgin Islands to side step this obligation. The US tax authority, the IRS, started proceedings against the banks for criminal conspiracy to evade tax.

Since 2008, private banks have paid in excess of $300 billion; just enough for it to hurt, not enough to put them out of business.

Private banks, in particular in Switzerland, have reacted by refusing to give any form of advice, which for many good private bankers eager to look after the best interests of their clients is frustrating.

However, with a major source of valuable information gone where can the UHNW community go for relevant advice.

They are too small a community to make it worthwhile newspapers keeping them informed as to their options, and the specialist magazines are predominantly industry specific and not client centric.

There is therefore a need for digital platforms such as BConnect Club to serve both communities; providing the UHNW community with a one-stop shop of deals, luxury products and service providers with an opportunity to display their products and services without the reader being identified as having a need or interest, until such time as they are ready to do so.

Even when advice can be sought and given, it is not always easy to evaluate the advice being given or compare one solution with another. Each advisor comes with different jargon. Who do you trust?

Robin is looking to invest £4 million he inherited from his uncle. He could invest in a discretionary portfolio, a house to let, an equity stake in a friend's company, or a care homes fund. The choices are limitless and everyone has an opinion as to which is better than the other and why. It is just so very confusing.

To make matters worse for the vulnerable UHNW a sales pitch is often taken as independent advice. If Robin were to go to his banker Peter to ask what he should do with his inheritance, Peter is unlikely to suggest anything other than a discretionary portfolio because that is the only investment that makes him a fee and gets him closer to achieving his targets.

Moving forward

Once you have identified the need for an advisor, don't rush to reveal your need for advice, your identity or contact details. Make sure you have at least five to 12 positive 'touches' or validations before letting an advisor know you are interested.

These validations should include:

- Case studies of someone with similar goals to yourself.

- Good testimonials.

- Personal profile on LinkedIn that is aligned to your values.

> You want your advisor to know what your goals are and to do what they can to help you get there.

- Positive information from Google and Twitter.

- Information on the website that suits your goals.

- Information from the brochure that supports everything else.

- Recommendation from a trusted advisor.

- Referral from a friend.

- Adverts, corporate literature and events reinforce the message that this advisor may be suitable for you.

- Interviews, videos and PR are engaging and aligned to your values.

Only when you are happy with what you see and hear should you make your contact details known and arrange for an interview or go to one of their events. At this stage you will need to have your questions prepared, the relevant goals laid out and know what you are expecting from them.

Does your advisor have a good network?

One factor that is often overlooked in choosing an advisor is how well networked they are and how familiar they are with the expertise and knowledge of that network. As I will describe in greater detail in the pages to come, you need your advisor to be able to provide you with the level of service you want. You want your advisor to know what your goals are and to do what they can to help you get there. This should include referring you to other advisors in their network who can do for you what they cannot.

Sadly so many advisors are myopic about their area of expertise. They cannot recommend or refer their client to another advisor because they do not know enough about the advisors in their network and what they do for their clients.

I have frequently asked advisors what they would do if they were unexpectedly to receive £100 million. The advisor who can tell you what to do, who to go to and why, is going to be more valuable to you than the advisor who would not know where to start. Advisors may have been in the wealth industry for decades and be widely networked, but they need to understand the type of problems their clients face and how they can use their network to assist them.

As a UHNW individual you are in a minority and as such you are not well catered for in finding the information you need to manage your wealth and advisors. Newspapers need to appeal to a wider audience than the UHNW community, so they will not cover what the UHNW needs to know; tax legislation, offshore trusts and cross border succession.

There are a number of books the UHNW individual can buy and read to get started. There are also numerous events and clubs where they could learn more.

Building your Inner Ring of Confidence

Finding the right combination of skills and expertise in one advisor is not possible, so you will probably have to look to develop a team, your inner cabinet, in the same way as a Prime Minister forms his or her cabinet.

You need a team of advisors you can trust – but it has to be your team, not a dysfunctional group of experts all jostling for your attention and influence over you. If you allow your advisors to get out of control, you will be buffeted from one to another. They

> The inner cabinet always jostles for power. It will be the same with your team of advisors.

will confide in you about what they've heard in the marketplace about the others as they try to out-manoeuvre those of greater influence.

In all powerful courts, whether it is the court of Claudius, Henry VIII, or the Godfather, the inner cabinet always jostles for power. So it will be with your team of advisors – human frailties do not change.

And do not ignore the influence of family and friends. It is well documented that Cherie Blair was not keen on Gordon Brown, but he nevertheless managed to hang onto his influence over Tony. Yet there are plenty of examples in history where key influencers have not been so lucky.

I was working with Gustav on his tax planning when he and his wife came to live in the UK. His wife was a beautiful woman in her mid fifties. She had formerly been his secretary and had successfully separated him from his first wife by working late and going on business trips with him. She was also a jealous woman. When she saw that Gustav had a female advisor, my engagement was abruptly terminated. She was not going to let any female close to him, regardless of whether she was married or not.

Your inner Ring of Advisers can take a number of forms: an advisory board, trustees, or non-executive directors of the family business. From my experience this inner circle should be governed by an agreement, which should be formal and in writing, if the family is of substance. Everyone needs to know what their role is and what is expected of them. They need to know who is part of the decision-making process, who needs to be informed and of what, how long the notice period is, and when a decision has or has not been made. They also need to know when and how someone new can be made a member of the inner circle and the procedure for demoting a current member to the outer circle. The management of your inner Ring of Confidence is at the heart of the GFOS Protection Packages.

You may think this is over-complicating matters, but it is lack of formality that leads to disputes, tensions, gossip, back-stabbing and distrust. This is damaging to all involved and leads to poor decision making.

Of course, a UHNW founder can do with his or her money as he or she chooses and change the rules as he or she sees fit. A founder needs to keep his or her advisors on their toes; if they don't the advisors will try to align their founder into serving their interests, rather than his or her own.

Charles is a self-made millionaire. He has a team of advisors who meet once every month to discuss the management of his business and investments. One month he asked them to consider the sale of part of his business which was underperforming. Harry is a corporate lawyer and very much in favour of the sale – he can see what professional fees he'd make from it. John is the corporate financier, he knows of a suitable buyer and can also see professional fees on a sale. Josie is a tax lawyer, she's not convinced that a sale is the right thing to do; she'd prefer that the head office relocate to the Cayman Islands to improve returns. Michael is a chartered surveyor, he would prefer that the offices from which the business operates should be sold and leased back to provide funds for expansion.

Charles needs to make up his own mind about what he wants to do; he must not allow his advisors to bamboozle him with their own agendas. He needs to instruct them carefully engaging them only in the details; the strategic direction must be his. If he is not mindful of the self interest of each member of his inner cabinet, the management of his business and his investments will become a burden – and a headache.

Forming a family office

Although many authors track the history of the family office to the families that emerged out of the Industrial Revolution such as the Rothschilds, Fords, and Carnegies, I'd like to suggest that family offices have been in existence since the moment a founder had sufficient money to warrant employing people to look after it.

For example, there are estates scattered across the UK. Fortunes have been made and invested in houses and farms, which were run by offices usually located on the estate. The issues they had to face then were similar to what a family office faces now; it is just that the assets of the estate were in the case of a landed estate illiquid whereas today they are often liquid.

> If a UHNW engages high calibre people as advisors rather than as employees, he must always be on guard; they will have ulterior motives.

The reason why most founders of family fortunes form family offices is to employ people who do what the founder tells them to do; as an employee their only source of income is from the family office. They are not independent with another source of income and therefore do not have an alternative agenda.

The only difficulty is that independent advisors (if they are any good), earn a lot of money in private practice. If a UHNW individual wants to employ someone, he will either have to match what they could get in private practice or employ someone of a lesser standard.

Stephen is a first rate tax lawyer with impressive experience. He can earn upwards of a million pounds a year in private practice. To recruit someone of Stephen's calibre, the founder of a family fortune must be prepared to pay Stephen close to what he could get in private practice. This makes running a family office very expensive for a UHNW individual if he wants the best calibre of people working for him. However if he engages these people as advisors rather than as employees, he must always be on guard; they will have ulterior motives.

What does a family office do?

The main functions of a family office are:

- Integrated and holistic investment and tax management.

- Neutral and truly independent advice that is aligned to the family's goals.

- Management of the family's fixed assets, including insurance and security.

- Succession and leadership management.

- Communication between family members.

- Central administration.

Whether the family is passive in its investment management, using independent portfolio managers, or whether it is active, co-investing with other families direct into projects, will depend on what the family wants and who they employ or engage to look after their best interests. If a family wishes to co-invest they should be very certain that their advisors are experienced corporate financiers who know how to do due diligence – there are so many people who have all manner of investment opportunities. They talk the talk, but many are inexperienced and too immature to be trusted to 'walk the walk'.

The most important functions of a family office are reporting, risk management and co-ordinating the advisors. There are numerous software packages available to help run a family office, which is why it is staggering that up to 80% of all single family offices still rely on spreadsheets. Computer software programmes can save a family office hundreds of man-hours and provide versatility, accuracy and usefulness in times of economic change. However, not many make full use of what is available to assist them.

A Half Way House

Most UHNW families, even rich ones, cannot afford a dedicated personal family office and therefore look for a solution which recognizes their need for control while at the same time being mindful of the need for the arrangement to be formal, relevant, effective, efficient and reasonable.

Sheith M was one of the wealthiest families in the middle east who had a good team of advisers, who he wanted to be in control of his trust, which he had established in the Bahamas. He had formed a trust, not for tax mitigation purposes because he was not required to pay tax, but for purposes of asset protection out of reach of opportunistic personal creditors, smooth succession on his death, providing for people who he wanted to benefit and when, and privacy.

We worked with him in forming his own personalized, Protection Package. He was so pleased with it and how it made him feel in control, we have adapted it for our UHNW clients so that can be in control, through their advisers of their wealth and their inner Ring of Confidence.

Privacy and confidentiality

The other reason why families want to manage their wealth in their own family office or their own Protection Package is to maintain and secure privacy and confidentiality.

If wealth is managed by a public institution, there is no control over who gets to see the details of the family's wealth. In all institutions there is staff turnover. These employees are not contracted to and managed by the family. The family will not know what screening and monitoring has been done of the staff and what leakage of information could occur once a member of staff has left.

Confidentiality around the details of wealth is of exceptional importance. With information can come all manner of criminal activity, from theft to kidnap. A family must do everything it can to avoid the leakage of information to protect them and their family which is now increasingly difficult with worldwide exchange of financial information as from 2017/2018.

> When a family is in dispute over who is to take the lead on decisions, wealth goes into sharp decline.

In 2008 an employee of LGT Bank in Liechtenstein stole details of clients' accounts and, after leaving the bank, sold them to the governments where these clients were resident. This became the catalyst for a worldwide crackdown on secrecy, but just goes to show how dangerous a former employee who has had access to private and confidential information can be. I do not approve of undeclared bank accounts, but neither do I approve of stealing and selling private information.

Now, reliance for information from rogue employees is not necessary. Tax authorities across the globe simply rely on their local legislation to collect and exchange it with the country in which the owner is tax resident.

Passing on decision making to the next generation

The founder also needs to be mindful as to how his or her inner Ring of Confidence will serve the family, when the founder is no longer there to keep them in order. The next generation may not be as strong or as effective in making decisions as their parent, but they need to be. The founder will have to make it very clear on his demise or incapability as to how and who is to make decisions in the family. If no one is directing the inner cabinet of advisors, the advisors will take over the decision-making. When a family is in dispute over who is to take the lead on decisions, wealth goes into sharp decline. This type of family anarchy leads to great distress and misery and should be avoided at all costs. The only winners are the advisors.

Joshua was the founder of a multimillion pound investment management company. It had two classes of shares, A shares which were quoted on the stock market, and B shares which were left to his son David and two daughters equally on his death. When Joshua died David wanted to cash in his share of Joshua's investment management company. His sisters insisted that the restrictions on his shares devalued his shareholding, and so he took action against his sisters and his company in court. As the family argued for several years, the price of the quoted shares sharply declined. Family rows are expensive and damaging and must be avoided at all costs.

Does your advisor share your values?

It is important to know what your values are and try to choose advisors who share them. If you do not have a values statement you need to craft one. Simply write your values on Post-It notes and arrange them in order of priority. These values should be referred to whenever you make a decision. Having a value statement makes decision-making easier and much more consistent. It also makes choosing an advisor easier. My values are integrity, caring, respect and transparency.

> Whenever possible you need to choose advisors who share your values...

Wherever possible you need to choose advisors who share your values, in this way you are more likely to be able to trust them. You should also be aware of what type of decision-maker you are. Are you decision averse? Are you comfortable with uncertainty? If so you may be too hasty in making decisions.

If you have a tendency to be hasty you should be alert to the need to do more due diligence. If you are decision averse you should remind yourself that there comes a time when further due diligence will not make matters any clearer and you have to take a leap of faith.

Do you and your advisor share the same interests?

What do you like doing? If you follow football, work with people who have a similar passion; if you are a family man, gravitate to others who like spending time with their families. If you're going to spend a lot of time working with someone to achieve your goals then the more you can bond over similar interests the more pleasurable it will be.

I have often observed advisors meeting clients and the first thing they say is 'did you the see the game on Saturday?' There is no time wasted while they work out which game they were referring to – they just know. Another group of advisors and clients are all avid watchers of Jeremy Clarkson and cars and it's essential that they don't miss that week's episode. If they did they wouldn't be able to take part in the banter the following week. Other people like discussing politics, watching tennis, and so on.

The other advantage of sharing the same interests is that you get to know each other better on the race track, at the tennis matches, at the football games or wherever and share knowledge, news and views that are not work-related.

What other things may be relevant?

Other influencing factors will include political persuasion, religion, culture, family, ethics and habits. It is not necessary that you share the same religion or culture, but it is essential that you understand the religion or culture of people you work with and for. I went to see the head of a Muslim community and I wanted to know whether, as a woman, I should extend my hand to shake, whether to cover my head and whether it would be preferable to wear trousers, rather than a skirt.

Marion, a lawyer, has a client who is a Middle Eastern gentleman. When she or any of her female colleagues visit Saudi Arabia, they show their respect by wearing an abaya, a top-to-toe black robe worn by the women of that country.

It is also necessary to know what would be offensive, for example showing the soles of your feet is deeply offensive in the Middle East, not honouring your business card is disrespectful in Japan, and offering pork to a Muslim or meat to a Hindu would be unwise.

The choice of a trusted advisor is a personal matter, so personal issues need to be taken into account.

For more tips on how to get there, including notes and videos please scan the code or copy the link
http://www.garnhamfos.com/wysr-extras/chapter-4

In the next chapter we will look at Getting More, it is not enough to know where you are going and how to get there, it is also imperative to know where are the opportunities and threats, so that you do not lose what you have got and make the most of it.

Chapter 5
Getting more: UHNWs

Chapter summary:

- Types of asset and alternative investments.

- Acts of God and other disasters.

- Don't let disputes get out of control.

- Tax avoidance comes at a price.

- Manage liquid wealth as you'd manage your business.

Asset classes

I am not an investment manager, I am not regulated by the Financial Conduct Authority and do not give advice, for that you need to go to someone who is. However, you need to know the different asset classes – the costs I will deal with in chapter 10. You also need to know the extent of what your advisors do for their clients. You are unlikely to be directed to an investment opportunity which that organization does not cover. This is why goal setting must come first, and only thereafter check to see if your advisor can take you where you want to go.

Mark was interested in investing in EIS (Enterprise Investment Scheme), which is tax efficient and can bring enormous enjoyment, but is also risky. He asked his investment manager about investing in one, only to be told it was too uncertain. Interpreted another way, the investment manager did not have any EIS investments and didn't want Mark taking funds to another manager to invest in EIS opportunities!

Jane wanted to invest in property in London, so she asked her investment manager for his opinion only to be told that London property was overpriced. Why? Because it would mean Jane taking money out of her portfolio and investing elsewhere so her investment manager would then have less assets under management (AUM). But don't get cross with your investment manager. Just remember that turkeys don't vote for Christmas.

A quick overview

Sophisticated investors may find this summary of asset classes somewhat facile, but sometimes it is good to strip out the jargon.

Traditional asset classes.

- **Cash and fixed income.** In essence safe loans and money in the bank. Even this asset class is not without risk, Treasury will play around with currencies, and some companies, institutions and governments can default. It can be argued that countries in the European Union have less flexibility to raise taxes or print money to cover their debt liability and we all thought that institutions like Lehman Bros were as safe as houses until 2008.

> ...we all thought that institutions like Lehman Bros were as safe as houses until 2008.

As a rule of thumb, cash and fixed income is capital preservation and liquidity; it will not give a good return and hardly any income given the current low rates of interest, it is however good to have some cash or fixed income investment in a portfolio, because if your higher yielding equities and alternative investments are not ready to sell and you need income, cash and fixed income can come to the rescue.

Cash and fixed income can also provide much needed funds for the acquisition of distressed investments (assets selling for below their market price), because the seller needs the money quickly.

- **Equities**. A share in a business enterprise that usually takes the form of shares in a company or other form of business enterprise. Unlike debt or cash, and depending on the terms of the equity, if the business enterprise is successful, then the value of the share goes up and the chance of getting a distribution or dividend increases as well. Equities are liquid or illiquid depending on whether you can buy them in a market or Exchange. In order to be 'listed' on such an Exchange the company must comply with strict rules, the Stock Exchange Rules. Shares with a 'full' listing on the Stock Exchange are relatively transparent and can be sold relatively easily with the market determining the price. Market value in this context means the price that a willing buyer will pay from a willing seller.

  The junior markets such as the Alternative Investment Market or AIM also provide a market for the sale of shares and demand compliance from their companies. This market is primarily for smaller and less mature companies, and invariably offers greater return for more risk. They are safer and more liquid than private equity or shares in companies that are not listed on any Exchange. Then there is the choice of investing in large cap (companies that are well capitalised), and small cap, (those that are less well capitalised). Although small cap companies are more vulnerable, they can also produce higher returns, but my advice is **never** invest in any company whether listed or not, or small cap or large cap, without **doing due diligence**, or having some qualified person do it for you.

- **Check out whether the government gives incentives for investing in certain types of companies**. The EIS (Enterprise Investment Schemes) and SEIS (Seed Enterprise Investment Schemes) are extraordinarily generous to encourage investors to invest in small- to medium-sized companies and can as a result take much of the risk out of investing in these companies. But only invest if you know what you are doing or take advice.

Alternative investments

Interest in alternative asset classes has risen considerably over the past two decades as a result of poor returns elsewhere. In response a large number of boutique investment houses have cropped up, with a wide range of asset classes on offer, many of which are illiquid, including:

- **Hedge funds.** These cover a multitude of types, but in essence they take out debt to invest more. This leads to a magnified return when markets are good, and uses hedging techniques to manage the down side of the risk. Before the crash in 2008 many were producing 20% returns. In recent years only the top quartile is producing this rate of returns, and others are struggling.

> Before the crash in 2008 many hedge funds were producing 20% returns.

- **Structured products**. In essence these are very clever ways of making money – but you need to be absolutely sure who is making profits out of whom. For example, if you have exposure to a high interest rate on a contract, or currency exposure, it may suit you to do a swap. But if you don't have the risk in your business or personal portfolio, a swap makes little or no sense for you. In each case it is absolutely imperative that you take independent advice – your interests may not be aligned with those of your advisor.

- **Co-investment.** Or going into a project with others. This is talked about more than it's actually done. Co-investors need to get to know each other and build trust, which is why BConnect Club hosts investor events for UHNWs who'd like to co-invest so they can get to know each other and the investment opportunities of their peers.

- **Commodities**. Such as coffee, tea or any other material of great interest to a wide number of investors.

- **Precious metals.** Such as diamonds, gold and platinum that are similarly of interest and are often taken as a sub-class of commodities.

- **Real estate.** Such as land, warehouses, private residences and such like.

- **Infrastructure.** Such as roads and pipelines. This is often taken as a sub-class of real estate.

- **Collectibles**. Such as art, antiques and jewellery.

The real problem with alternative investments is that they are illiquid and there's no easily available market, so if you need to sell, you need to find a willing buyer. If you need to sell in a hurry, then you'll get a poor price for your investment as a distressed sale. Many of the investments require managing, such as private equity or properties, and you need to know when is a good time to buy and to sell, which I'll deal with in chapter 10.

Avoiding losses.

The primary role of any advisor is to make sure you avoid making losses. Nigel is a successful investment manager and his philosophy is not to make losses – if you make one you'll struggle to provide a decent return on investments while at the same time making up lost ground. His philosophy was not to go for stellar returns, but stick to avoiding losses.

There are six ways in which losses can be incurred:

1. Disasters and fraud

There are natural disasters (or acts of God), and then there are man-made disasters such as theft, burglary and fraud.

I arrived in the Bahamas a short while following a hurricane; trees were uprooted, walls smashed and roofs were lifted off houses. The force of a natural disaster is awesome. I also know of one man who lost a wife and child in the tsunami. "It just came out of nowhere," he told me.

Of course, you cannot live your life terrified of disasters because you'll never do anything exciting or fun, but be alive to the dangers. One husband and wife, Tim and Maureen, put all their savings into a boat to sail

> ...bad things don't always happen to other people...

around the world. They should have taken more care to avoid the areas where pirates were operating. Maureen not only lost their life's savings, but her husband and she nearly lost her own life as well.

Accidents happen if you are going to do dangerous things: think about the consequences, bad things don't always happen to other people. Not everyone is nice, they have lives to lead and mouths to feed and think it is their right to steal from others; burglaries and theft happens. I seem to have been very lucky; I live in an apartment that has access to the roof via a fire escape. One year I was having some decorating done and the door to the fire escape was open.

A cat burglar had stolen a computer and jewellery from a home a few doors down and was making his escape across the roofs, the police had been alerted and a helicopter was following him. The cheeky burglar was delighted to find my fire escape door open. He slipped into my apartment, much to the surprise of my decorators, dropped off his swag in my son's bedroom, took the lift down into the basement, where he took off his black jacket and sauntered out of the front door straight into the waiting hands of the police. However, it was at first difficult to make a conviction stick because he had no swag and the man they caught was not wearing a black jacket, which was how everyone had described him, even though they later found his black jacket in the basement!

I was working in a law firm where the conveyancing partner at the end of corridor kept himself very much to himself. He had a decent practice, but he was not a stellar performer. We always assumed that his wife had money because he lived a very comfortable lifestyle in a big house in the country. Surprisingly he left, and a number of assistants took over his practice. One astute assistant noticed that a large number of cheques were being made out to Coutts following the successful completion of a house sale. The monies that that should have been paid to his clients as the balancing charge were being sent to his own account. He'd been doing this for years. He was jailed and struck off the solicitors register.

Luckily you can find insurance to cover most forms of disaster, but you need to be careful as to what is in or out of the small print of your insurance contract. For example, you may have insurance that covers you for accidents while mountaineering, but if you fall when climbing Everest and you don't have cover for mountain recovery there will be no helicopter to come to your rescue and no one else will either!

2. Dispute resolution

This is often called litigation when it involves going to court, but a cheaper alternative is mediation or some other form of dispute resolution. Disputes cannot always be avoided and mediation is not always better than litigation. A good advisor will tell you how and when to fight and when not to. If you are up against a tricky opponent who is unlikely to do what a mediator says, it may be quicker and cheaper to litigate without going to mediation first. Ideally you need an advisor who has common sense and does not fuel your emotions to rectify the injustice done against you. Revenge, as they say, is best eaten cold.

A good advisor will not only be able to tell you how and when to fight, but also what the likely outcome is going to be. If they are any good, he or she will manage you to make sure you don't let the litigation run out of control.

> A good litigator will not only tell you how and when to fight, but also what the likely outcome is going to be.

The worst type of litigation is families at war. From my experience this is invariably fuelled by emotion and a deep-seated sense of injustice. In a domestic dispute, no matter how good a litigator is, it's not always easy to manage the parties. Some won't even try; instead they milk the dispute for every last penny.

David wanted his considerable fortune to be used for charitable purposes and set up a trust for his children John, Andrew and Margaret, who he optimistically thought would work together to fulfil his wishes. During the last ten years of his life, John had worked for David in his charitable activities as Andrew once had before he married and went to live abroad. David had little respect for either John or Andrew, who he frequently reprimanded in front of others, including his advisors. The apple of his eye was Margaret, whom he openly adored. He was impressed with her intelligence and good sense and spent many hours discussing his ideas with her.

On his death, following a short, but intense illness, the pent up frustrations John and Andrew had with their father erupted. They wanted a greater share of their father's estate and so worked tirelessly to conceal assets and write off debts owed by them to various projects. Margaret also worked tirelessly to unravel what they were doing. Several of the advisors suggested that the family engage a mediator to resolve their concerns, but they could not even decide where to meet or who to appoint, and it was clear that neither John nor Andrew would agree to what a mediator would determine. Margaret having discovered that some assets had not been disclosed, was now suspicious of everything and would not let any stone to go unturned. This dragged out matters and annoyed John and Andrew. The family feud could only be resolved through the power of the courts. It ordered John and Andrew to disclose all assets and Margaret to take a more pragmatic approach if the estate was not going to end up in the hands of the advisors. It took over five years to resolve this family feud with the cost running into many millions of pounds in fees.

The family dispute in the Thyssen family is another well documented example. When Thyssen got married for the fifth time, he chose a Spanish beauty queen, following the settling of most of his assets in trust for his fourth wife and her children. As his beautiful new wife produced children, she became anxious about the assets that could never be inherited by her children. Thyssen was persuaded to take action to dismantle the trust he'd created. This led to a litigation feeding frenzy that lasted for many years, only to be finally resolved by mediation. Soon thereafter Thyssen died. Again millions were paid in legal fees.

> ...the litigation feeding frenzy lasted for many years, only to be resolved finally by mediation.

There are numerous cases of such litigation. From my experience of seeing how it tears families apart, I would advise any founder of a fortune however big or small, to set up a wealth owning structure which incorporated good governance principles; where decisions are not taken by a unanimous vote, where officers can be removed and replaced , where there are no protectors non binding wishes and reserved powers and disputes can be resolved without getting out of hand. Also make sure you employ the best advisors possible to avoid a family dispute. Good advice at this level is worth its weight in gold, furthermore if you are in a dispute, and the parties can resolve their difference through mediation, then mediate. If not get the best litigator you can and resolve it as quickly as possible.

3. Divorce

There is one sure way of avoiding a divorce and that is not to get married or indeed in many countries not to have a permanent relationship. But we are human and we like being in relationships regardless of the consequences.

I can think of too many blood-chilling stories to write them all down here, so I'll just give you two examples here.

Alex was a successful City lawyer who was due to inherit a substantial estate from his father with extensive land and a shoot. His passion was his family history and it was always agreed that he would save to pay for the upkeep of the house when inherited which would enable him to write the family history.

After the death of his father, the day came for him to move into the estate. His wife Anne Marie refused to go with him, saying it was cold, uncomfortable, draughty and damp. Then she started divorce proceedings. On the divorce she scooped the savings, leaving Alex with his beloved estate, but no money to keep it maintained and no hope of retiring to write his family history.

> ...she was told that she should agree to a low settlement that would get paid to avoid the need for expensive global tracing litigation...

On the flip side, Wendy had been married for 24 years and helped her husband build his business into a global empire. He was non-UK domiciled but UK resident, and so had his assets in numerous trusts around the world. He left Wendy to go off with his personal trainer and started divorce proceedings. The first thing she was told on taking advice was that she should agree to a low settlement that would get paid, to avoid the need for expensive global tracing litigation if he refused to pay her what a judge ordered.

She was advised by another expert that an order could be enforced across Europe. She got as large an order as she could and then pursued her former husband with an experienced commercial litigator. So don't be afraid to get a second opinion and don't be afraid to use experts from a different discipline to give you fresh eyes on an issue.

Of course, one is always inclined to feel sorry for each person who confides their story to you. Only when you hear the other side do you get a better feel for who is being fair and reasonable and who is being a gentrified thief.

4. Taxes

As they say, there are only two certainties in life – death and taxes. As a fellow of the Chartered Institute of Tax I know a little about tax and I have to confess that for many years I thought it was fascinating. I remember being at a party many years ago where a young man tried to chat me up. He asked me what I did. I told him I was a tax advisor, to which he replied "would you take me home?" Indignant I replied: "Tax advisor you clot. Not taxi driver!"

I also wrote as a contributor for the *Financial Times* on tax and trusts for twelve years as well as for another publication which is not around anymore. In the first few years, I was convinced no one was reading my articles, so I tried to work words or phrases not common to the world of tax and trusts into them. In one article I managed to work in a recipe for nettle soup, and in another a polka dot bikini. The more fun I had in writing the more prominent my articles became, which was ironic really.

There are many, many taxes, and the rates and types of taxes vary from country to country, but in essence direct taxes come in three types:

1. **Tax on income**, whether that is active, such as employment income or from a business or partnership such as being a lawyer, or passive income such as dividend income on a share in a company or interest on a loan or debt.

2. **Tax on a capital gain.** If you buy a plot of land and it has increased in value by the time you come to sell it, then you will pay tax on the capital gain, against which you can in certain circumstances set off any losses.

3. **Tax on gifts, or death.** If you give money to a child, parent or friend during life or on death, you may need to pay tax on this gift. In some countries, the more remote the relationship the higher the rate of tax.

There are a number of reliefs. For income tax there is an annual personal allowance, and different rates depending on how much income you get a year, there are also allowances for capital gains tax, such as relief for your principal private residence. There are also reliefs for taxes on gifts, such as on gifts made more than seven years before death, and gifts to charities.

Indirect taxation is the tax on purchases, such as Value Added Tax (VAT), which is added on to most purchases. Again there are exemptions such as for children's clothes and food, which are considered essential.

Legitimate tax planning is knowing what reliefs there are and taking full advantage of them. If you're about to buy a second home you are given two years from the date of acquisition to elect which you want to treat as your principle private residence. This is legitimate capital gain tax avoidance because you are using the relief in the manner in which it was intended.

Marcia lives with her husband, Tom, in the country. They wanted to buy a pied-à-terre in London, which they did. They spent very little time there, possibly two or three days a month. They thought they would enjoy it for ten years and then probably sell it. It was rocketing in value so it made huge sense to elect for this to be treated as their principal private residence, because this was making the greatest gain and would be sold first. The fact that they hardly spent any time there was irrelevant, they could use the election to determine which was their primary residence.

> DO NOT EVADE PAYING YOUR TAXES. HMRC in the UK has draconian powers against banks, other countries and you...

Tax evasion is of course illegal. This is when taxes are due, but you don't declare or pay them. My strong recommendation to anyone living in a developed sophisticated country: DO NOT EVADE PAYING YOUR TAXES. HMRC in the UK has draconian powers against banks, other countries and you, to find out if you are cheating. Furthermore the powers granted to an inspector are far more lethal than powers given to an investigator into a murder and there is little or no right of appeal or compensation if they go after you; even if they find nothing. However, if they find that you are deliberately and knowingly evading tax they will have no qualms about throwing you into jail.

Using reliefs in a way they were not intended is called tax avoidance and governments across the world are keen to curtail it as best they can. Gordon Brown when he was Chancellor was messianic in his eagerness to stamp out all forms of tax avoidance by seeing in which way reliefs were being used, and if used successfully but in a way which was not intended, ordered legislation to be drafted to block any gaps. The UK now has more tax avoidance legislation than any other country in the world other than India.

The biggest gaps however, are the ones between one country and another, which the UK government can do little about. Lady Thatcher swept away exchange controls in June 1979, and thereby allowed money to move freely between countries and with it the opportunities for planning.

One good example of tax avoidance using different countries are the arrangements put in place by companies like Amazon and Starbucks.

The directors of every company have a duty to maximise its returns to shareholders. This means that if there is a way to save tax and they don't then they could be in breach of their duties to their shareholders.

If a company is global, where it bases its intellectual property is entirely up to that company. It is perfectly simple to set up a company, say in the Cayman Islands, and transfer to it the company's intellectual property rights. Cayman does not charge income tax. If then every business that operates in a high tax jurisdiction is charged

> ...there are treaties between most countries that determine which country has the 'taxing rights' so you are not taxed twice...

a fee for using the logo and doing business according to that license which wipes out its profit, when the company wants to pay a dividend to a shareholder, they borrow the money locally so as not to bring the profits from the Cayman into a country where it will be taxed.

The situation is more complicated when you are dealing with people, not businesses. If you are not living in a country and were not born or domiciled (which is different to residence) in a country, then you will probably not pay tax in that country. However, you can live in one country and visit another on a regular basis and find you are being taxed in both countries, which is called double taxation. More often than not there are treaties between most countries that determine which country has the 'taxing rights' so you are not taxed twice, but there is one notable exception.

Governments always have time for taxes on business, income and capital gains, but the taxation of gifts and on death is not only incredibly difficult, because of the different laws in the different countries, but also it is such a low priority of government time.

So a massive warning, the fact that you did whatever you could to pay all taxes due and had no intention to avoid tax is no defense.

Tax authorities are ruthless, have deep pockets and care little for the discomfort, expense and time taken to defend a demand for tax.

With the introduction of the automatic exchange of information under the Common Reporting Standard introduced by the OECD, which become operative across the world in 2017/2018, tax authorities will know who owns what finances and where. They will also know who has set up trusts, how much wealth is in them and any persons who are of significant influence on the trust and trust assets.

Tax authorities around the world have been told that if a trust offshore has significant wealth, and has a Protector, then there is prima facie evidence that the trust is a sham and can be set aside.

This may be a sweeping and wrong decision but it may be enough to sweep aside privacy and start an investigation. This must be avoided wherever possible and I have worked for many years looking for and finding solutions.

I was involved with a tax plan which saved inheritance tax on homes. It had been given the blessing of several leading Queen's Counsel and seemed watertight, even from a change of legislation.

The Treasury did not like it; it was too successful. So the Treasury introduced an income tax charge to counter the inheritance tax advantage and thereby killed it overnight.

However, many innocent people got caught up in structures they could not unravel without significant tax payments when asked for a time frame and incentive to unravel Treasury simply said, that those who play with fire should not complain if they get their fingers burnt.

We have seen the same harsh attitude from the Treasury on offshore structures used by non UK domciliars who own residential homes in the UK. Over the years from 2014 to 2017 the tax benefits; capital gains tax and inheritance tax have been removed for those who wish to retain the benefits of a non UK domiciled status, singeing annual taxes, and for those wanting to unravel their structures no leniency, understanding sympathy or concern. The same attitude is evident for those trying to mitigate their tax, don't complain if we change the rules to catch you.

This is to my mind an abuse of power and retrospective taxation and should be curtailed by appealing to the European Court of Justice.

5. Investments that crash

You buy an investment because you hope it will increase in value, and you sell an investment in the hope that you will reinvest in a higher performing investment.

No matter how much due diligence you do before you invest you cannot predict the outcome, to that extent it is a gamble. Seasoned investors say you should only ever invest in what you understand and with people you know and trust, but even so people can be unpredictable and not what they seem, they can disappoint and change. An enormous amount of time and money may go into predicting trends, sectors and securities that seem undervalued to get a better return.

> Seasoned investors say you should only ever invest in what you understand and with people you know and trust...

Risks and returns are correlated; taking greater risks can lead to greater returns, but can also lead to greater losses. The innocent investor can often get swept away by hype, and emotions – gold is soaring, get in now before it's too late. This property with planning permission (which is just a formality) will rocket. This new technology project if you buy now will be the next Facebook. Affordable housing with solar panels that can power all their electricity needs will transform the lives of the poor in emerging countries, buy now to help the poor across the world. A new cancer drug, it only needs one more round of testing and it will beat ovarian cancer, just look at the tests on mice... And on it goes.

It is an exciting rollercoaster that engages many bright and eager UHNWs, but it is not for nothing that one-third of UHNW individuals within five years of a liquidity event have lost one quarter of their wealth no matter how substantial it is.

In most cases, like time, money when it's gone is GONE.

6. Wasting assets and excessive spending

One thing I want to make clear is that if your money is yours you can do with it as you like and if you want to blow it all on the 3.30 at Kempton Park it is your decision to do so. But when it is gone it is gone.

There is a well-known saying that the two happiest days of a boat owner are the day you buy the boat and the day you sell it. Owning a boat or a plane is like setting fire to bank notes, fuelling a boat or a plane is eye-poppingly expensive, not to talk of the repair bills and staff. But if you enjoy the boat or the plane and can afford it, go for it.

Personally, I hate queuing for anything and feel a thrill about being singled out for personal attention. I was stranded in the airport in Jersey waiting for the fog to lift. We also had to wait for the plane to leave Gatwick and arrive in Jersey before we could get back. A friend of my client had a plane on the island that had not gone out in fog before, and he invited me travel back with him. Leaving my fellow passengers behind, I travelled to the private plane part of the airport and we were whisked off in a matter of minutes. As we arrived at City airport we were met by a chauffeur driven car and I was at my desk in London before the flight from Jersey had taken off!

Some expenditure is excessive. I occasionally shop in Marylebone, where I have found a little boutique which sells nearly new clothes. The owner says that she gets her clothing, shoes and handbags from chauffeurs, hotels, domestic staff and women who just buy too much stuff and either give it away to their domestic staff, leave it behind in the hotel room because they cannot carry it, or like to think they are getting some money back from the second-hand shop following a hasty purchase.

> Buying for the bin is a great way to keep our economy bubbling along...

Buying for the bin is a great way to keep our economy bubbling along, but if it is your money, just remember that if you are buying in excess of what you're making, your buying is eroding your capital and you are making losses.

Liquid wealth needs just as much managing as illiquid wealth

It is tempting to spend when wealth is liquid and there is no reason why you should not, but like most things in life you cannot have your cake and eat it. With liquid cash you need to be aware of the dangers and make sure you have set your goals to do what you want to do with it and not what others suggest you may like to do. Do you want to end up with little or no monies to pass on to your children and grandchildren?

In the next chapter we look at delivery, you need to value the service or product you want, only then should you think of what it is costing. It is often said of fools, that they know the cost of everything and the value of nothing. If an adviser charges by the hour, it is not the rate which is important, but how many hours will they take, how much experience do they have and how busy are they.

Chapter 6
UHNWs: delivery

Chapter summary:

- Value and the cost of advice.

- The ins and outs of investment management.

- How to make trusts work for you.

- Professional advisors and what to watch out for.

- Other advisors.

Most advisors do themselves no favours by focusing too much on cost and too little on value. If you are going to get the most out of your advisor and your wealth you need to be very clear about the value of their advice as well as how much it's costing you.

Advisors come in many shapes and forms, but I think it is helpful to split them into the following three groups:

- **Investment managers**: bankers, brokers, private bankers, and fund managers etc.

- **Professional advisors**: lawyers, accountants, tax advisors, trustees.

- **Others**: reputation advisors, insurance, security, estate agents and other service providers.

Investment managers

What is investing?

An investment manager's job is to manage investments and this can be either passive or active management. The active investment manager is looking for trends in the market, undervalued assets and such like, and to minimize losses by diversifying and using hedging techniques. For this they employ analysts, brokers, traders and managers. In addition, they need a team of specialists to select the best stocks, and strategists, and lawyers to create financial products. This then needs to be sold to the investor, for which they need a team of managers.

The passive investment manager selects a diversified portfolio that is reviewed on a regular but infrequent basis, such as once a year.

Investment management, whether active or passive, is not a science. It does not follow rules that can be used to predict the future. It is an art because it is dependent upon people, and as we know, people are fickle and unpredictable.

Active management.

I think the most helpful way to describe trends or spotting under-valued assets is to draw your attention to Malcolm Gladwell's book *The Tipping Point*. This is a study on what goes into making a 'trend'. He breaks it down into three factors:

- The law of the few.

- The stickiness factor.

- The power of context.

The book's introduction starts with the example of Hush Puppies – the classic American brushed suede shoes with a lightweight crepe sole. In 1994, Wolverine, the company that made Hush Puppies, was thinking of phasing out the brand as it was only selling 30,000 pairs a year. Then for no apparent reason they became hip in the clubs and bars of downtown Manhattan, and by the autumn of 1995 the trend began to take off. In1995 Wolverine sold 430,000 pairs of Hush Puppies.

Trends such as these Malcolm likens to an epidemic, they start off small and then dramatically take off. If you had shares in Wolverine in early 1995, you would have made a fortune. Investment managers are looking to buy investments that are about to tip up, and to sell investments that are about to tip the other way. But just as no one could have predicted the rise of Hush Puppies, no one can predict the future of the markets. There are a lot of analysts and strategists who look for early signs, but very few make the right call over and over again, and even these stellar investment managers have poor patches.

Finding the growth and managing the losses.

There are three ways in which the active investment manager is looking to find growth; finding Wolverine shares, finding them in 1995, or finding the person who can find Wolverine shares.

- **Finding an investment that is undervalued**. At its simplest an investment manager is looking for stock with potential, particularly stock that hasn't been noticed by other people yet. There are some very talented people who study economics and sectors, and pore over balance sheets and Profit and Loss accounts to spot when a business is likely to take off or tank. They can see when the cash flow of the business is weak and that it may need to sell an asset, whether litigation is pending, or whether it is cash positive and looking to buy. Although, their guess may be significantly better than mine, it is still a guess, albeit educated.

> People tend to hang onto something that looks good and ditch investments that are going south...

- **Timing.** The collapse of Lehman was a shock to many of us, but experts who knew about its distressed companies were aware that Lehman was in a dire financial position as early as 2006/7. Yet it still took another eighteen months before it actually fell. Timing, as they say, is everything.

When a stock is tanking, will it recover or should you stay in for more pain? Who knows? As a stock soars, should you take profits now and reinvest in something that is looking cheap, or wait a little longer to get an even bigger slice of profit? People tend to hang onto something that looks good, and ditch investments that are going south; but this is not always the best strategy.

- **Choosing the right manager**. In days gone by, this was simple. You had lunch with your mate in the City and, because of the inside knowledge he had, he'd be able to tell you which stocks to pick (usually over large quantities of alcohol). He'd know which company had won what contracts, which were about to take over a competitor, and who was employing whom, all of which had an effect on the price – once that information filtered out to the general public. Insider trading has now been banned and there are all sorts of rules as to closed periods and non-disclosure.

  Picking a good manager is also an art. Some managers can perform exceptionally well for a few years and then go off the boil, maybe because of a divorce, illness or sheer self doubt. You can stay ahead of the game by switching managers in a timely fashion, but it is just as hard to predict when a manager who has gone through a rough patch will come back on to old form as it is to know when to sell on a rising tide or which stocks to pick.

How does the active investment manager make his money?

Your active investment manager, like your banker, does not earn much money by holding onto it and doing nothing. He makes his profits when money moves – or when it is surrounded by layers. In this regard an investment manager is a bit like the tax man. Until you have realized a gain, you will not be taxed.

There are essentially four main categories of fees that the investment manager charges:

- **A fee for managing the investments**. This is the fee that every investor is told he is paying to the investment manager for managing his investments. It is usually between 0.5% and 1.5% which no one really minds because the investment manager is an expert and needs to be paid.

- **The fee for making the transaction**. The investment manager will make a fee not only on the sale of the stock, but also on the purchase of the replacement stock. Let's say your investment manager sees the price of a stock flying, and decides to 'take profits', he gets a fee for that sale. Then he spots a stock that looks as if it is undervalued and he buys it in the hope that that will rise; the investment manager earns another fee for this purchase.

- **Fees to a third party**. The investment manager may not be an expert in all areas of investment and therefore buys into a fund where the fund manager has a good track record. The investment manager will be paid a fee for making the introduction, which is often called a 'kick-back'. This is where conflicts can arise – the question that needs to be asked is does the investment manager choose the fund with the best track record, or the one that pays the largest kick-back to the investment manager?

> ...does the investment manager choose the fund with the best track record or the one that pays the largest kick-back?

This is the area that is the most difficult to track and monitor and an area that leads to the greatest concern amongst investors. Of course, most investment managers take a balanced view, if he chooses funds with the lowest returns because they produce the higher kick-backs, the performance will be poor and the client will be dissatisfied. The investment manager needs to keep his client, or he will get no kick-backs at all.

- **A fee for doing well**. If an investment manager has done well over a particular year he can award himself a performance fee. This varies from investment manager to investment manager. Some say they will charge a lower fee if they don't perform well, but if they outperform they'll charge a higher fee. The trick is in how they measure success; what do they measure themselves against? There are numerous benchmarks that measure good performance given the economy or market or whatever. If the benchmark against which performance is measured has gone down, and your investment manager has not made such a large loss as the benchmark, you could pay a high performance fee even though your investment manager has lost money. It is for this reason that many investors are only interested in absolute returns, which simply means, 'have I made money or lost money in the currency in which I do business.'

In total, active managers will be charging their clients around 5%, but it will be hard for any one investment manager to tell you precisely because your money has very often been pooled with other money and therefore the fees cannot be accurately assessed.

Is my active investment manager so focused on beating the market that he forgets I may want peace of mind?

The primary role of a bank is to be a safe haven for your money. It also provides you with the means to move your money around, cheque books, and credit and debit cards, accounting and lending money, whether for business or personal usage. However, banks do not make much money from general banking business, so they are now active investment managers as well – trend spotters.

> How do I know when my investment manager is acting in my interest or his own?

The danger point is when a bank has your money, because you have to put it somewhere, and then your bank manager starts to sell you their investment management services and products as if they were advising you independently. In most cases your bank manager is paid a commission on how much of your money he can **actively** manage, so there is a clear conflict of interest between the bank and the client at the point of delivery.

How do I know when an investment manager is acting in my interest or his own? There are four things every UHNW individual needs to ask:

- **Is my investment manager or his or her organization good at spotting a trend** or opportunity and is this advantage of benefit to me after the costs of paying the analysts, brokers, negotiators, lawyers and specialists?

- **The layers being suggested to me**. Are they of any benefit to me?

- **How does the bank make its money** to pay for these expensive professionals?

- **Is the person who is advising me on my investments** also the one who is employed by the investment manager to sell these products?

The reason why there have been such high levels of dissatisfaction from UHNWs with investment managers in recent years is that some have been mis-selling in the guise of giving advice. May I remind readers of the fines that most banks have had to pay for mis-selling, (see chapter two, Part One). This is why the Financial Conduct Authority has been clamping down on the banks and investment managers.

Active or passive investment management?

Returning to value, rather than cost, not everyone buys clothes or food because they need clothes or food, they usually buy because they want something.

Investment managers who are in the upper quartile are probably beating the market even after fees, but is it just about beating the market? Surely it has a lot more to do with peace of mind. If I am fearful or anxious but I know there's someone at the end of the phone who's keeping an eye on my portfolio 24/7 and who knows what's happening in the world economy and how it could affect my investment portfolio then this will give me peace of mind. This is of value to me, regardless of whether they are beating the market or not, and I am prepared to pay for this service.

If this is what an investor wants from an investment manager, then this is where the relationship manager should be focusing his or her efforts in providing an excellent service.

If, however, the client is cynical about the value of active management and their ability to outperform the market, then a passive investment management may be more appropriate. There is no right or wrong, it is a personal decision based on what you, the investor, wants to do, knowing all the risks and non-aligned interests.

From research done by Scorpio, 56% of UHNWs use active fund managers, the rest either do it themselves or are passive. To test whether your investment manager is truly passive or active you need to get an honest answer about how they are remunerated.

Is my investment manager a wolf in sheep's clothing?

The most important question to ask of your investment manager is 'how are you getting paid?' You need to know what their bonus depends on. Do they get paid more if:

- **They get more assets under management (AUM).** Then they will do everything they possibly can to make sure you keep your money invested with them and that you sell properties, businesses, art or whatever to do so – beware.

- **They do a transaction**. This could lead to market churn. The market as mentioned above is made up of willing buyers and willing sellers. There are in any one year 50% of winners and 50% of losers; it takes two to tango.

- **Their client invests in a product, whether it be one of the banks or one from a third party**. Are they paid more for one product than another? If the answer is yes, you are in a very tricky situation if your investment advisor is also being rewarded depending which products they put you in. This is a clear conflict of interest and a client in this position should be wary. If you don't understand and you are being told to be quick – be careful.

Layers

There are many professionals who'll encourage you to have layers around your investments. As a rule of thumb, layers should only be introduced if they provide a benefit that you can understand and want. I have set out as an example trusts to give you a flavour of how layers can be of benefit, and why they need to be understood.

Trusts

As a world leading trust specialist, it has to be said I am fond of the trust – but I have also seen it create phenomenal family disharmony and pain.

A trust is a three-way obligation. Let's take Jacob. He has a wife Mary and two children Tom aged six and Melissa aged three. He is advised to set up a trust so that on his death Mary is provided with an income and on her death the capital passes to Tom and Melissa. This has the advantage that Mary, if she were to remarry, could not leave his fortune to her future husband and their children and the capital is preserved for Tom and Melissa.

Jacob needs to appoint trustees, whose job is to manage the investments in the best interests of Mary, Tom and Melissa. But who should he choose?

The relationship manager at his bank may at this point suggest Jacob appoint their trustee department who could do Jacob's probate as well as fulfill the role of trustee. However, a word of warning, I have seen probate charges of up to 1-2% of the monies of the entire estate, whereas a lawyer may just charge on time. If the wealth is significant the difference could be colossal. The bank will also charge an annual trustee fee. When they are trustee they are then poacher and gamekeeper.

The role of trustee is as **owner** of the funds. This means that if Mary, after the death of Jacob, asked the bank appointed as trustees to give her the money, they could legitimately and legally say no. Furthermore, they could start piling the wealth they're managing into funds that make the bank a kick-back,

> There are many excellent bank trustees, but this conflict of interest has to be remembered.

or into structured products that give the bank additional fees. Provided the trustee considers what they're doing is in the best interests of the beneficiaries and there is power to benefit under the trust from the investments (which there usually is), then they can do so. And they don't have to give any reason to Mary or her children. Furthermore, Mary will have no power to remove the bank as the trustee unless the power has been reserved to either her or someone else to do so.

The advantage for Jacob is that the money will not find its way to Mary's future husband, but the flip side is that if the bank is the trustee, provided they are acting in the best interests of the beneficiaries, there is nothing the beneficiaries can do to stop them doing whatever they want within their power under the trust deed.

There are many excellent bank trustees, but this conflict of interest has to be remembered. If a family needs some capital, for which there is a power in the trust deed to pay this sum, the trustees may be more inclined to refuse making this distribution because it would mean losing precious assets under management and possibly a bonus for the trustee.

It was for this reason, among others, that I pioneered an area of law I called family governance which makes sure control is with the settlor's trusted team. I encouraged families to form their own company to be the trustee, who could then contract with a professional trustee such as a bank to provide the day-to-day administration. In this way, if there was any concern with the bank, the trustees could simply terminate the contract with the bank that was administering the trust assets and enter into a contract with another.

Trusts and tax planning

Trusts have been used extensively for tax planning for UK resident non-UK domiciled individuals of which there are 144,000 in the UK. The law gave special income tax, capital gains tax and inheritance tax reliefs for wealth held in trusts offshore set up by people who were UK resident (i.e. they spent a significant amount of time in the UK, but were not domiciled there). A person is non- UK domiciled if their parents did not belong to the UK at the time of their birth and their emotional home remained outside the UK.

> Trusts have been used extensively for tax planning for UK resident and non-UK domiciled individuals.

To take advantage of the capital gains tax and income tax reliefs, these non-UK domiciled UHNWs needed a trust, the trustees of which needed to be resident not only offshore, but in a jurisdiction that recognized trusts such as Guernsey, Jersey, Bahamas and the Cayman Islands. Banks of all kinds set up branches in these jurisdictions to offer trustee services to people such as these UK resident and non-UK domiciled people as well as others resident in other jurisdictions who could also use trusts to legitimately avoid taxes. I use the words legitimately to avoid taxes, because legislations make it clear that this is the law, they are not using a relief to bend the law in their favour.

Where the trustee needs to be resident abroad, rather than appoint a professional bank trustee I would advise families to set up a special purpose vehicle such as a company in the Bahamas which could then act as a trustee and take all the main decisions in the Bahamas. The trustee would then contract with a professional trust administrator, such as a bank, to provide trust administration services. The decisions were therefore kept separate from the administration and investment and avoided what could otherwise be a conflict of interest.

Queries then arose as to who should be the owner of this special purpose vehicle. Of course it was worth nothing. A trustee may own the assets in its name, but not for its benefit, so what appears on the balance sheet is nothing: it owns these assets for the benefit of its beneficiaries. This does not mean that the beneficiaries can make any decisions over the investments owned by the trustees, they can't. The value of this vehicle is in the power of the directors to make the decisions. The power of the shareholders is to remove and replace the directors and thereby remain in control of the management and investment of the underlying assets.

My solution here was to suggest and draft a new law, which I presented to the Bahamas government, and they accepted. This became The Bahamas Executive Entity Act and was passed into law in December 2011. This act creates a legal entity which, provided it owns nothing of value, such as the private trustee company, it has no value. The purpose of the vehicle is to make decisions, and therefore does not need to have all the onerous obligations imposed on it that would apply if it was an entity which owned value. I called it the BEE for personal reasons and I believe it is doing very well.

> Offshore trusts made the UK a very attractive place for foreigners who've been able to live here and pay very little tax on their worldwide wealth...

Having the Trustee separate from the investment manager and the trust administration services provides a much improved service from both. This is because they have to report to someone who has the power to remove them.

In the 80s and 90s offshore trusts were set up by the dozen by UK resident and non-UK domiciled people. The reliefs were not introduced to give a tax break to rich foreigners to entice them to come to the UK. They came into being after World Wars I and II in order to increase the tax reach from UK domiciliaries. However, as people have become more mobile, these reliefs made the UK a very attractive place for foreigners who've been able to live here and pay very little tax on their worldwide wealth, much to the chagrin of Gordon Brown. During his years as Chancellor he fervently tried to erode the extent of these reliefs.

The rules are now so complicated and the erosion of privacy so extensive, I advise anyone who is a non-UK domiciliary and has an offshore trust that has not been reviewed for more than a year to get an opinion as to whether you are tax compliant. Furthermore, I would trust only an expert in this field with sufficient professional indemnity cover to advise you. 'I didn't know I was doing anything wrong' or 'I took tax advice and they never said I'd have to pay any' – these excuses just don't wash with HMRC, which is why it is so important for you to ask your inner Ring of Confidence for ongoing advice, because you cannot know whether or how much danger you are in, and you need to know before HMRC knocks on your door to enquire.

For those non UK domiciliaries who want to protect their privacy, live in the UK and for whom the primary tax concerns are inheritance tax (currently at 40% on death) they can set up trusts onshore, with UK resident trustees, or bring their offshore trust onshore, provided they were neither domiciled nor deemed domiciled at the time value was transferred to the trustees to be held in trust. We can assist you with finding the best solution and advisers for you.

Professional advisors: lawyers, accountants, tax advisors, trustees etc

It's not always easy to know when you need advice. You may have some investments that are not what they seem and in danger of causing a problem, you may not be aware that your succession plan is flawed and you may be unaware that your insurance is inadequate. Usually these flaws are not discovered until it is too late, which is often expensive and stressful.

UHNW individuals set up family offices so that someone can find out where the gaps are and plug them ahead of time instead of finding out the hard way. As a rule of thumb, things like insurance should be reviewed every year when it comes up for renewal, investment managers should be reviewed every three years and succession plans should be reviewed every five years.

The first thing you need to do before going to a professional advisor is to decide what you want to do and to try to articulate it. This should have been done when you were setting goals. Then you need to do your research on what is achievable and relevant. You need to be clear on the time frame and what will they want from you. You should get all of this together before your first meeting.

Engaging a professional who charges by the hour

Clear instructions are always a good start, but not always easy, especially when you are going to an advisor to seek advice. It is always tricky evaluating what is achievable before you've been given advice.

There are a lot of clients who go to several advisors before picking the one they want to work with. This is called a beauty parade.

When I was in private practice at Simmons & Simmons, I noticed a pattern with how some of the wealthiest families engaged me and my team. They would usually come to the meeting with their key advisor. Each of them later said:

- Their key advisor would be able to evaluate my level of experience and knowledge.

- They'd watch the body language between my team and their key advisors to see whether we could work well together.

Having discussed the problem that needs a solution, a strategy needs to be mapped out. However at this stage the professional advisor will want an engagement letter with terms and conditions, and you will need to disclose some personal details, for which you'll want privacy protection.

It is not at all uncommon that a new relationship begins with something small. The trouble is that something small, like a lease extension, won't be carried out by the same advisor who will handle the big job, e.g. your succession plan. These jobs will be done by very different advisors in the same firm. Don't feel you need to have one firm for all your professional requirements. However, there are advantages to using fewer rather than more firms. Using one firm keeps leakage of confidential information into the public domain to a minimum. It is a balancing act for which there are no easy solutions and no rights and wrongs.

Controlling the time spent by the professionals

Stay in control of the time professionals spend on your matters by asking the following:

- Do they charge by time?

- In what blocks of time; six minutes, ten minutes?

- How do they capture their time; on a recording system? Many firms now have a computer programme that measures time and they have to account for the matter on what they are recording their time. The flaw in this system is that the advisor could leave the clock ticking as he has a five-minute chat to an associate, a quick chat to his secretary, a brief telephone call on another matter, or a coffee or comfort break.

- Is the advisor a master of his time or does he let interruptions master him?

- How often does he report and what do the reports look like?

- How does he organize his work, does he plan and allocate an estimate as to the time each block of work should take?

- How does he bill? How frequently and with or without a narrative?

What has always ceased to amaze me is why more UHNW individuals do not insist upon an estimate and demand that the advisor stick to it, the letter of engagement is after all a contract, but it rarely seems to be treated like one.

> ...the letter of engagement is after all a contract, but it rarely seems to be treated like one.

The Law Society does not insist that its solicitors bill by time. It allows for a whole variety of variables to be taken into account, including value of the work to the client, the urgency of the matter, and the size of the transaction. At the moment most advisors charge the same rate per hour whether they are working at midnight or midday; the same rate per hour whether they are dealing with a transaction of several thousand or thousands of millions; they charge the same whether it has to be delivered in a day or a week.

Knowing this, the craftiest of my clients would always set ridiculously tight timetables knowing that I could not charge beyond the hours there were in the day. If he could I'm sure he would have insisted that we only work on his matter between the hours of seven in the evening and seven in the morning when he could be fairly confident that his advisors would not be distracted by other things.

Another client insisted on a fixed cost and then caused it to overrun by two weeks. I charged a pro rata addition to which, after some irritation, he agreed.

Although not true of all, most professionals could charge in a manner which was fairer on themselves and more caring for their clients. The only reason why they charge by the hour is because it can be measured, although not very accurately.

A more sensible system and one for which there are systems, is to agree with the client a matrix of measures, including all the variables, the size of the transaction, urgency and value to the client, which also includes time, but is not restricted to it. It takes much more effort to set up before any work is done, but the client has a better idea what they're paying for and can see the value in it.

This takes me to two of my many exasperations with professional advisors. They know all the features and costs of what they do and none of the benefits and value to their clients. This again takes me back to my culture of care. If the professionals could genuinely see the benefit and value of the work they were doing for their clients they would:

- Be more profitable.

- Not get bogged down in minutiae that make not a halfpenny difference either way.

- Focus on what is important to the client and point this out.

- Focus on what should be of importance to the client and why.

- Genuinely advise and not just regurgitate what the law says, leaving it to the client to make up his or her own mind up about what to do.

More about this in the next chapter.

Other advisors

There are so many advisors and specialists it is hard to know where to start and where to stop. Some advisors are necessary, such as tax advisors and bankers, and some need to be managed, such as private bankers, lawyers, security, reputation risk, personal shoppers, yacht brokers, personal trainers and on and on.

There is no short cut to research and reading the small print. If something feels wrong don't do it. If you are being hyped about something, or made to rush, think again.

A word on concierge services which are so popular at the moment. Engaging the services of a butler who is not exclusively there to serve you is often going to lead to frustration. The party with the wrong flowers, the staff issues that were never resolved... The secret to any type of concierge, even more so than any other service, is to know your client. If you're not working exclusively for your client, this lack of knowledge will inevitably cause problems. There are two solutions: manage your expectations, don't think you can reach the stars when you have only paid to get to the moon, or employ someone who works solely for you.

Whether you want an advisor or not, who you choose and why, is a personal decision. All I would say is 'choose wisely' because when wealth is gone, it is gone.

For more tips and videos please scan the code or copy the link **http://www.garnhamfos.com/wysr-extras/ chapter-6**

In the next section we look at how to maintain a good relationship with your adviser, how to make sure they remain focused on you and your concerns – and genuinely care for you.

Chapter 7
Retain and maintain: UHNWs

Chapter summary:

- Use SMART goals to assess your wealth advisor.
- Why you have to do your homework.
- If the relationship's not working – fail fast.
- How to be a good client.
- Tell your advisor to communicate in language you understand.

What is measured gets done

You have set your goals; you know what you want to achieve and what advisors you need or want to help you get there.

However, your job is not over once you've identified the advisors you need and have engaged them; it has only just begun. You must now communicate what you want from them, set a time line, benchmarks, processes and systems of checks and balances. You have to stay at the helm; working with a new advisor is no time to sit back.

Only when the relationship is going in the right direction at the right speed and everyone is doing what they are supposed to do can you afford to have a break. It's a little like getting the ship out of harbour and off in the right direction. On taking on any new advisor, it is up to you to set the tone and the standard that you expect.

You must have an honest conversation about what you want, expect and when it will be delivered. Be friendly, honest and open, but remember you are the client; your advisor needs to prove that he or she can deliver the benefit they promised before you start to trust them. He or she may have promised to 'take the tedium out of managing your wealth so you can enjoy it', but until the advisor has proved that he can do so safely **do not trust blindly that they will deliver what they said.**

In particular you need to clearly set out the following.

- **Your goals.** Communicate clearly the specific goals that you want the advisor to deliver. Have an open discussion. You should also be clear about what will happen if those goals are not met. Don't compromise or your advisor will not respect you. You may need to set priorities – it may not be possible to implement the whole plan immediately – but you will need to know what the journey looks like and what to expect when. If the outcome is dependent on unknowns, set out how far you can go before the unknown becomes known and make it clear that at that stage you want a review. Take the example of litigation: you can make a claim, but until you see what the counterclaim is you have no idea how long the litigation will be, or how costly; so you need to plan and budget up to the counterclaim and when the counterclaim is served plan and budget for the next phase.

  > Don't compromise or your advisor will not respect you.

  Also make it clear how you want to communicate with your advisor: by phone, email, message or letter. Don't assume they'll know how you like to communicate. I tend to miss voicemails, so tell everyone not to leave them. Make sure that the advisors know who all the stakeholders are. Is it just the client, or also their personal assistant, wife, child, or trusted advisor, who need to be copied in? Again they will not know until you tell them.

- **How will progress be measured?** How frequently should the advisor report, in what manner and in what form? All reports must be fully understood, if they are not they are useless to the client as a yardstick. Again remember that you are the client, do not let your advisor bamboozle you or bully you with jargon: it is your wealth he is referring to and you are the client. To repeat what I have said before, you need to make it clear to your advisor that not only do you expect a good service, but you will not tolerate unjustifiable excuses for poor performance.

- **Is it achievable?** The short answer is, it depends. Consider the example of a house developer. The client works with the developer and they decide on a schedule of works and a time line. Let's say that the builder, as he begins to work, discovers subsidence. At that time you would want him to stop work and discuss the extent of the subsidence and what needs to be done to put it right with you, so you can both look at how it will affect the timeline and the price. In the same manner any advisor should be told that the moment anything unforeseen crops up that will affect the timeline or expected outcome, they need to down tools and talk to you about it. Make it very clear that you want to be told all bad news immediately. There are so many advisors who, the moment an unexpected issue presents itself, start immediately to try to resolve it without discussing it first with the client.

If the unexpected issue is complicated, then the advisor needs to learn to communicate complex issues in a manner that you will understand. If reporting on unexpected issues does not happen, then you, the client, should

> Advisors are inclined to use jargon to explain why they have failed to deliver.

expect your advisor to deliver what they promised and in the time set for delivery as agreed. Again, don't trust your advisor blindly.

When you are told bad news, does it stack up? Advisors are inclined to use jargon to explain why they have failed to deliver. You need to know how genuine the excuse is. You need to demand to know and understand what the problem is and why it is going to cost more and take more time to deliver. If you are peddled excuses you do not understand, you have a choice; either you trust blindly (which I do not recommend), or you demand to know more. You also need to do some research of your own.

Unacceptable excuses are those that relate to other clients: 'I have been in meetings', 'a client of mine had an urgent issue', 'I had to go abroad on urgent business'. This does nothing more than tell you that other clients are more important, which is the antithesis of a culture of care. Of course, it must be remembered that your advisor is human as well, and issues do crop up that are beyond his or her control. Everyone must be prepared to give and take a little. It is when the frequency of excuses diminishes the quality of service that you should think of finding another advisor. If your advisor simply does not care for you, sticking with him or her will not make it any better. Of course, you need to be reasonable, your advisor cannot be expected to outperform the market all the time or never to make the occasional mistake, but if you have set your goals carefully and you have researched what is achievable you should know when genuine unknowns pop up, or when you are having the wool pulled over your eyes.

- **Is it relevant**? At this stage you need to be wise, you need to convey to your advisor sufficient information about yourself and your goals to enable them to advise you properly. The difficulty is knowing what is and what is not relevant. You should not jeopardize your privacy too early. Your advisor needs to earn your trust and if he or she does not, you must be prepared to go elsewhere, having divulged as little as possible.

> A good advisor will not only tell you what information is relevant, but also why.

The difficulty at the beginning of a relationship is knowing what information is relevant and what is not. If you are engaged in a succession plan, your advisor will need to know what and to whom you want to leave your estate and in which jurisdictions you have assets. Let's assume John has had a daughter with a dancer, for whom he has provided, and his wife and her children know nothing about her. In continental Europe it is public policy to leave a substantial part of your estate to all your heirs, including any illegitimate children. If John was of continental European descent or had property in continental Europe, he would need to disclose the illegitimate child to his advisor. However, if he had no connection or property in continental Europe and all his assets were in the UK, he need not. A good advisor will not only tell you what information is relevant, but also why.

- **Is it timely?** There may be many things you want your advisor to do. However, it is not wise to give a new advisor a long shopping list at the outset. See first as to whether he or she can perform on a small matter before committing to something more substantial. Don't be too open about your wider plans until you have seen whether your advisor can deliver. Be friendly, courteous and respectful, but know the difference between these attributes and the quality of service you expect and for which you are paying.

Do not give excessive praise to an advisor who has done nothing more than what you are paying them for, but do give healthy feedback. Jane asked her investment manager to diversify her portfolio, to perform against agreed benchmarks, to notify her of any unexpected fluctuations in the market and report quarterly. At the quarter end, she set up a meeting with her investment manager. She said: "I asked you to diversify my portfolio within a time frame and with adequate reporting, which you have done, thank you. But I also asked you to report on any unexpected fluctuations in the market. The unexpected takeover of one of my investments has made quite a difference to the price. I would have expected you to call me rather than leaving it to this quarterly meeting to discuss it." Jane's advisor has now been told what she wants. She will expect him to listen and report immediately in the future.

There is no short cut – you need to be knowledgeable

Information is readily available now, so make sure you know what you need to know.

Ask your advisor questions. From my experience the most basic questions usually elicit the most insightful answers because it means some thought has gone into them. However, don't just rely on what your advisor says. There may be gaps in his or her knowledge or they may be making excuses, or learning as they're going along. In Jane's case, she has now been told that the unexpected takeover of one of her investments has made a material difference to the performance of her portfolio for that quarter. Jane can then research that company to find out when it became known that a takeover was imminent. If her advisors have overlooked some material news, she wants to know why. Remember, they will respect what you inspect and knowledge is so easily accessible now.

> Information is readily available now, so make sure you know what you need to know.

The internet

If you come across something that could affect either you or your wealth, you can easily find out more using one or more search engines. There is an ocean of information available and a myriad of different ways and forms of explanation: Wikipedia, articles, magazines, advisors' newsletters, blogs, and so on. The only problem with this abundance of information is assessing whether it's reliable and, once you've found credible sources, knowing what applies to you. Say you have a pain in your back. If you read the article written by a surgeon you'll think you need an operation, if you read the article from the acupuncturist, you'll think the answer is needles, if from the osteopath you'll think you need manipulation and if from the personal trainer you'll think you need exercise, which is why ultimately you need an advisor to tell you what is best for **you**.

Being knowledgeable is fundamental to keeping your advisors on their toes. With knowledge you can ask searching questions and challenge why decisions were taken or not. Using your knowledge well ensures you get the best possible service. Furthermore, good advisors will enjoy teaching; they love an enquiring client. However, they do not like a client who is showing off; telling their advisors they are stupid. To get the best out of advisors you need to respect them, and if you cannot, switch advisors. But as I have said before, don't forget advisors are human, but they are also in business to make a profit. They are not therefore impartial; they will tend to advise you according to their expertise. Returning to my back ache analogy, if you go to a surgeon he is unlikely to recommend acupuncture, which is why you need to be knowledgeable and wary.

Reading material

It is tempting at this stage to suggest that you sign up to newsletters and magazines to keep up-to-date, but most UHNWs I know are bombarded with all sorts of material; they want it filtered to their preferences. They will know that within a pile of post may be something of relevance and interest, but do not have the patience or inclination to spend hours looking through what is irrelevant to find that one needle in the haystack. This is why so many UHNW families want a family office or a digital platform that can do this for them, like BConnect Club.

Aggregation websites

The real challenge for UHNW individuals is to find what they need to know. Pierre has been living in London for seven years. Before coming to London he lived in France and is French domiciled. He has a trust in Jersey. In the budget of a previous year the tax law on trusts changed, which affected him, but he did not know this. Why should Pierre start to search for details of a change in the legislation that affects him when he has no knowledge of it? To make matters worse, HMRC will assume Pierre knows about the changes in the legislation and will penalize him for not declaring this tax liability under the new legislation. Not knowing about the change to the law is no defense.

If for example Josie has been mis-sold a financial product, which is now taxable, how will she know that she should be declaring the tax on a product that she'd been told was not taxable? A lack of knowledge is dangerous in every aspect of wealth advice, not just tax.

> A lack of knowledge is dangerous in every aspect of wealth advice...

Martha, for example, is divorced from Grant. When they were divorced Grant had a good job in the City, he has now been made redundant and has applied to amend his maintenance provisions. Martha does not believe that Grant will remain unemployed and is advised by her lawyer to resist. This angers Grant who as a result decides that now the children are at school, she should get a job and start to pay for herself. Had she accepted what he was offering, she would have been better off. She is now facing having to find a job and years of bitterness with her former husband. Martha needs to be reminded that her divorce lawyer will not be making any fees by telling her not to fight. She should not follow the advice of her lawyer blindly – she needs to keep hold of her common sense. Grant cannot pay maintenance if he has no money coming in.

UHNW individuals like my friends and former clients Charles and James are inquisitive – but struggle to find the information they need to be sufficiently knowledgeable to keep their advisors on their toes. How can they find out about something which they may want if their advisor does not offer it as part of his service. To go back to my back ache example – how can Charles find out about what an acupuncturist can do for him if his advisor is a surgeon?

The UHNW individuals want to meet. They are invited to numerous events and opportunities, where they can meet others, but most have a price tag attached – whether asking for a donation to a charity, subscription or a product push.

I held a breakfast for some of my UHNW clients some years ago to ask them about their attitude toward co-investing. Ed said that fewer UHNW individuals were co-investing than wanted to, because they did not know each other well enough. To my mind this is a pity, wealth needs to move to be of value to the wider community, it needs to be invested in projects which can make a difference and create

employment. He said that he meets other UHNW individuals from time to time at events, but there was nothing tailored for what they wanted – to get to know each other sufficiently well to want to co-invest. There are numerous family office events, but when asked about them, the usual response was that the most useful time is the meetings in the lobby with other UHNW individuals; not from any of the talks for which they are ostensibly there to hear.

Your network

Making friends with other wealthy individuals is essential to learning how to manage your advisors and wealth. This is not because you are disloyal to your old friends; you merely need to make new friends with whom you can share opportunities and experiences. When Tom sold his business for £160 million he wanted to learn how to fly. He joined a flying school and went to their events where he made new friends with whom he could fly to France or wherever they wanted to go.

Most purveyors of passion investments; planes, yachts, shooting, art and so on, provide opportunities for their clients to meet. Hubert has always been interested in wine, but when his father died he could indulge his interest. He went on a wine tasting course in Bordeaux, organized by his favourite wine shop, served some of the best wines at a dinner for his new-found friends and was soon invited back.

> When you are new to liquid wealth you may need to make some new friends.

Another very popular way of meeting people over a long period of time is to join an investment club. These take many different shapes and forms. My advice, if you are not experienced in investing, is to join a club but be wary – investing direct is a long term commitment and you should not invest without full due diligence.

People prefer to meet people like them, without threat or danger. Indulging in a passion with others who share a similar passion is a great way to get to know people, but not everyone knows how to get started. At one meeting I attended for UHNW individuals, one gentleman openly stated that he sold his business five years ago, but his lifestyle had not changed. When asked what he would like to do, he said he would like to learn how to shoot. I suggested that he may like to join a shooting club.

Another popular way for UHNW individuals to meet is through charitable giving. The fund raisers are always on the lookout for people who are willing to donate and will give them privileges and priority treatment. The benefit of spending hours at committee meetings is to meet other people like themselves, with the same interests, concerns and issues.

Christine has always been interested in the opera. She approached the Royal Opera House to see how she could help. As a friend she was given a variety of privileges for gala performances and back stage invitations to meet the stars. Through this she met numerous other opera lovers with whom she went to La Scala and other opera houses around the world.

The scope of charitable work is extensive and can cover a broad range of interests and concerns, from the arts, ballet, opera, heritage buildings, education (both adult and children), health, projects abroad, victims of crime, criminal rehabilitation, animal welfare, nature, research and development, racing, and even fashion. The list is endless. It is not difficult to find interesting people through charitable work, and many, many people find it gives them fulfillment, purpose and a new circle to friends.

A strong network is extremely important. Without a strong network of like-minded people, UHNWs feel lonely and their wealth becomes a burden, not a pleasure. It is not at all unusual for a UHNW individual new into liquid wealth to want to give it all away, because they feel isolated and uncertain. A strong network is important: it teaches you how to enjoy your wealth and gives you new friends to share your experiences with. They should point out the traps too. But here I want to sound a warning bell.

Although you can look to your network to point out dangers and introduce you to opportunities, a fellow UHNW is not an advisor, so any advice or recommendations should be treated cautiously. A better introducer is your advisor, not your network. Nevertheless your network is important.

> It is important that you maintain and retain an advisor with whom you can build a relationship based on trust.

They can alert you to issues on which you need to seek advice or on which you need to do some research, but do not trust them blindly.

Don't put up with poor service

It is just as important that you maintain and retain an advisor with whom you can build a trusted relationship as it is for your advisor to keep you as a client. To do this successfully you need to be a good client.

I was recently approached by James, a UHNW individual. He wanted to take a distribution from an offshore trust and had instructed an accountant for some number crunching about whether he should rebase of not. The accountant promised to deliver by mid-February. He didn't. James pursued him. The accountant said he'd been busy on other matters and gave another deadline, which he similarly ignored. After much nagging he finally delivered the numbers with a warning that to rebase may alert the interest of HMRC, which simply confused James. The accountant had quoted an estimate of £800 and proceeded to deliver an invoice of £5,000 plus without any explanation, no reporting during the months of delay and no warning that the estimate was likely to be exceeded or why. This lack of care and high-handed approach to a client simply should not be tolerated. I told James to ask his accountant whether he wanted to keep him as a client, but to find himself another accountant regardless of the excuses.

Fail fast. If the relationship is not working with your advisor, and your trust has been damaged, terminate the relationship as soon and as painlessly as you can. It may involve you in some extra work and some difficult conversations, but you are the client and bad service is unacceptable – don't put up with it.

Being a good client

If your wealth advisor shows signs of being competent and caring, then put some time and effort into showing them how they can become the advisor you want them to be. Begin by giving your advisor feedback, whether they ask for it or not.

> If your wealth advisor shows signs of being competent and caring, then put some time into showing them how they can be the advisor you want them to be.

Any reporting or advice must be understood by you, or it is a waste of time or money. It is true that legislation and the movements in the markets can be tricky to understand, but remember that you are not in school. You are not a pupil who is less good than others in this subject. You are paying for advice and your advisor is being paid to advise you; this means that you need to know and understand what it is he or she is telling you. If you do not understand, your advisor must find another way of explaining it until you do.

Long letters filled with hard to understand legislation or market fluctuations are not about giving advice; the advisor is essentially showing off. It is accepted that your advisor may find his or her area of expertise of immense interest, but it is more than likely that you do not. This is why you have gone to him or her for advice in the first place. This does not mean that you don't want the five pages of explanation, you do. If his or her advice turns out to be faulty you need to know where the error lay and give it to another advisor for a second opinion. The explanation should not however be the letter of advice; it should be attached as a schedule. The letter should refer to the explanation in giving advice which should be a specific recommendation.

Advisors are often reluctant to give advice, because they fear that it may have unexpected consequences. This is like a doctor being afraid of prescribing a drug for fear that the patient may experience unforeseen or unexpected side-effects. The doctor should know that in prescribing the drug, you are likely to get better, if not he will have to think again. He does not fail to prescribe for fear that it won't work or that there may be unexpected consequences.

You are paying your advisor to give you advice and he or she may not get it right first time – we are all human and make mistakes. Usually the mistakes are minor and can be rectified with honest and open dialogue. If not and the wrong advice leads to a loss, this will be covered by the advisor's professional indemnity insurance.

There is no excuse for an advisor not advising – that is what they are being paid for.

Ask your advisor to communicate with you in a way you understand

Few advisors put themselves in the shoes of their clients, so you need to tell them what you want. As a first step you need to make them think about the value of their service to you. Why are you seeking his or her advice and what do you want to achieve at the end of it?

- Do you fear that HMRC will come knocking at your door, or would you rather pay as little tax as possible?

- Do you want to get good returns on your investments, or is it more important not to make losses?

- How important is it for you that your children retain harmonious relationships with each other following your demise, or is it more important to you to favour one child over another?

- How important is it to you that your home remains in the hands of the family, or that the children are well provided for, even if it means selling the home and its contents?

- How important is it to sleep at night knowing that your investments are being looked after by professionals 24/7 or would you rather trust the markets to come good overall and save on the fees?

There is no right or wrong, it is your money and your decision. Again do not let your advisor bully you because his or her goals may not be aligned to yours.

You need to remind your advisor what your goals are in seeking advice, and see the cost of taking such advice accordingly.

Remember, of course, that what you may value and what your advisor can deliver may not be achievable. If you want 12% returns on investments when the market is only making a 3.5% return it is simply impossible, unless you're prepared to take risks. If it is important to you not to make a loss, you need to accept a lower return. If you want to save tax remember the government is determined to stamp out any misuse of the legislation and will make life very uncomfortable if you are trying to use the legislation in a manner for which it was not intended. Your advisors will, on occasion, need to manage your expectations, but this must be clearly distinguished from making excuses for poor performance.

If your advisor is suggesting you do something that you do not understand, ask him or her for a case study that clearly shows the problem the client was wanting to resolve, and why following the advisor's suggestions resolved the problem. Case studies force your advisor to think about you rather than them. Because many advisors are not familiar with putting themselves in the shoes of their client, there may be some resistance to begin with. But if you want to build up a trusted relationship with your advisor, he or she has got to think about what you want to achieve and suggest ways in which you can achieve what you want, not what they want.

> Remember: you are the client, so behave like one. You deserve an advisor you can trust, but some of the responsibility must rest with you.

You should also ask your advisor to give you testimonials from satisfied clients. Again this will force the advisor to value their clients and listen to what they are saying, both good and bad. The good feedback they need to collate and use as testimonials, the bad they need to listen to so they can improve the service they give to their clients. All feedback is valuable. Of course you cannot expect any testimonial to be attributed to a particular client, because they will not want to breach confidentiality. However confidentiality should not be an excuse for not giving testimonials. **Remember: you are the client, so behave like one.** You deserve an advisor you can trust, but some of the responsibility must rest with you.

In the next section we look at Trusted Advisers, how do they treat you how should they treat you, manage your advisers well, monitor their activity and let them know you are watching, they will then serve you well.

Chapter 8
Trusted advisors: UHNWs

Chapter summary:

- How does your advisor treat you?

- Are you getting value for money?

- The many facets of wealth management.

- What's the best way to prepare your heirs to receive and manage wealth?

- Handle Advisory Boards with care.

The problem

The only difference between a UHNW individual and anyone else is that they have wealth and most people don't. Decisions have to be made about what to do with wealth – some of which can have onerous consequences if you get them wrong. If you don't pay your taxes you will be pursued by HMRC, but knowing what taxes you need to pay may not be obvious. Choosing a bank that won't go bust may not be an easy decision because finding the information on which to base a decision is not always easy. The same is true of advisors. Where do you go to evaluate who is best for you?

Furthermore, there are numerous options and different advisors say different things, plus they measure their success against different benchmarks, so it becomes almost impossible to compare one with another.

William sold his business in 2014. He paid off his mortgage and put the money in his bank. His bank manager, Mark, congratulated him on his success and invited him to lunch. Over lunch Mark explained how the bank would manage his money, how it could give him a strategy for charitable donations, advise on his succession, and create a trust for his children. William was not sure he wanted a trust for his children, but Mark seemed to think it was a good idea.

In the evening William went to a concert with Max, a friend who had been a banker, but who was now working for a multi-family office. During the interval, William told him what his banker had said. Max warned him not to commit himself too quickly and too extensively with the bank. "By the way," said Max, "did you know that bank was fined a huge sum of money by the FCA for mis-selling?" He suggested William visit his firm the following week to see what they did for their clients.

William is now confused, but he makes an appointment to see Max the following week – after all he did pay for the tickets for the concert.

The following morning he takes a call from a Karen, who he does not know. She congratulates him on the sale of his business and asks him whether he would be interested in investing in property. "There's nothing like bricks and mortar," she says. William says he's looking at options with his bank and a multi-family office. Karen is quick to point out the fees charged by banks and multi-family offices are extortionate and that he'd be better off investing direct into bricks and mortar. "You only pay one fee when you invest direct."

> One-third of newly liquid rich individuals lose a quarter of their wealth in the five years following the liquidity event.

As you can imagine, the more people who get to hear of William's good fortune, the more confused William will become about deciding what to do with his newly liquid wealth. He fears that there are traps and opportunities in all options, but doesn't know what they are.

The problem for William, which he probably didn't know at the time, was that when he converted his business into liquid wealth he gave up a business that he knew inside out for the business of managing his wealth and advisors about which he knows nothing. This transition can be extremely stressful. This is why one-third of newly liquid rich individuals lose a quarter of their wealth in the five years following the liquidity event.

Furthermore, like any other business, it cannot be left to manage itself. In time, of course, you begin to find your way around and you distinguish the obvious wolves from the innocent sheep, but you are always at the mercy of people who want to advise and assist for a fee.

It is for this reason that many UHNWs feel lonely and find it difficult to adjust to being wealthy.

On average it takes ten years after a liquidity event to feel comfortable that you are not going to lose it, and to get over the guilt of having liquid wealth. It takes a further ten years to start enjoying it. So don't leave it too long before you cash out!

Trust has to be earned

Advisors are much more comfortable when they can just 'get on with it', but that is not always in your best interests. As I said in chapter one, your interests may not be aligned with theirs. You have to be very sure that your goals are aligned with those of your advisor or you may find yourself in a position where you don't want to be. You need to remind your advisor that you want to know what is going on, and want the bad news as well as the good as it occurs, not when the bill is delivered.

Trust has to be earned and needs to be developed over many small steps, not giant bounds.

Is your advisor intimidating you?

Advisors don't often realise it, but they intimidate their clients. They have degrees and post-university training, and often they have their certificates framed and hanging over their desks. They speak at international conferences, are frequently too busy to take the calls of their clients, and are surrounded by eager enthusiastic assistants. Furthermore, they are keen to tell you that they have spent years advising clients from around the globe and that you are just one of many. They are very smartly dressed and are confident in their area of expertise and fluent in their industry jargon.

But don't forget that you are the client and for all their learning, jargon, expertise and knowledge they are there to **serve you** because you are paying them, and they need to understand what it is you want and make sure to deliver it.

Even when you have found someone who can assist you in achieving your goals you still need to take measured decisions and not let your advisor rule the roost. It is your money and you can decide what it is you want to do. Your advisor is there to assist, to point out where the traps are and where there are opportunities to be found, but it is still your decision that matters.

You must not trust your advisor until he or she has earned it.

Are you getting value for your money?

From my experience, it is not always true that you get what you pay for. Certainly the more reputable the organization the more training the staff are likely to have had, and the more rigorous will be their attention to keeping them up-to-date and well-informed, but if you need niche services you may have to go to boutiques to find the relevant expertise.

Craig is half Italian and half Malaysian, but lives in England. His father Giuseppe is getting elderly and thinking about making succession arrangements. He has been a successful importer of Italian foods to the UK and uses a well-known City law firm for all his business dealings, but the City law firm does not handle succession work. Giuseppe has blocks of flats on which he is earning an income in both Italy and Malaysia. Who should he go to for advice? First he needs to know that this area of law is immensely complicated and he will require English, Malaysian and Italian lawyers.

Giuseppe could start by researching who is knowledgeable and has written about in cross border succession, in particular English/Italian cross border issues. This area of expertise is likely only to be found in a boutique firm. If a law firm has no experience in this niche area, their advisors will be learning at Giuseppe's expense and may still overlook some material issue or practice that could make all the difference.

No substitute for knowledge

Education, education, education has been the mantra of many politicians for many years, and it's an important one. With knowledge your left brain is better equipped to warn you of dangers, avoid mistakes, choose advisors well and instruct them about what you want.

The problem is that the wealthy are a minority. They need to make decisions others do not need to make. What they need to know is therefore of little interest to others and for the majority is boring. There is no newspaper or magazine that is dedicated to keeping them informed about what they need to know to find advisors and investment opportunities. This is why you as an UHNW individual need advisors who genuinely care for you to keep you informed about what you need to know.

Owning wealth has many facets

The range of information about which you as an UHNW individual need to have more than just a passing knowledge is vast. To give you some idea:

- **Investing,** passive, active, direct, indirect, listed, unlisted, regulated, unregulated, real estate, leasehold, projects, sectors, trends, private, public and so on.

- **Structures,** companies, foundations, partnerships, trusts, contracts, LLPs, cell companies, companies limited by guarantee, SPVs.

- **Legislation:** what is permitted in which country and what is not. This varies from country to country and between countries, and affects everything from the speed you can drive your car, to the monies that a bank must have to cover its losses.

- **Case law,** there is case law on most things: acting in consort, mis-selling, contract, trust, patents, trademarks and so on.

- **Taxation,** whom do you need to inform or fill in forms and by when? There are different types of taxes; stamp duties on land sales, income tax, capital gains tax, estate taxes, gift taxes, value added tax, rates, and corporation taxes and these vary from country to country.

- **Treaties.** There are treaties between countries on everything; for example, whether a will is valid in another country (India is one country that has not signed such a treaty). Most countries have signed double taxation treaties between other countries that determine which country has the taxing rights and how to share revenue. In certain areas you would expect countries to have treaties, but they don't. Very few countries have treaties on estate taxes on the death of an individual with assets around the globe because the countries have very different ways of passing wealth from one generation to another.

- **Litigation.** Knowing when and how to litigate: resolving disputes, when to arbitrate, mediate or go to court, when to settle and when not to settle – all of this is notoriously complex. You need a lawyer who can assess your case and know when to fight and when not. Lawyers who fight regardless of the likely outcome should be avoided.

- **Protection.** You need to know when and how to protect yourself and your assets or business. Is your insurance comprehensive enough? Do you need to pay for personal protection or protection of your reputation? How do you protect your image? When and how do you go about protecting an idea, a trademark, or a brand? When and how do you enter a non-disclosure contract? What do you do if someone breaches an agreement?

- **Family Governance**. Who is going to make the decisions about your business, in your trust, over your art collection, in your foundation and with regard to your family?

- **Succession.** Should you leave everything to your children and, if so, when? Who should have control? How should that control work? When should changes be made? What and when is the best way to communicate this to the next generation?

- **Philanthropy.** Should you give to charity or engage in impact investing, or set up a foundation to do what you want? How do you go about setting up a foundation? Which charities should you support and which should you avoid? If you set up a foundation, who do you trust to be on your board? When and how much should you distribute and to whom? What powers does the Charity Commission have and how do you remain compliant?

- **Impact investing.** Many wealthy individuals are erring towards impact investing as an alternative to philanthropy. Instead of giving and forgetting, impact investing is about investing in companies that do good works, but where the donor remains accountable. These companies can extend across all the areas covered by philanthropy: health care, education, the arts and developing countries. The investment can be just as valuable to the recipient as a donation and in some cases even more so, because something is demanded of them in return. In most cases an investee can give a return in some way or another and feels far more engaged in so doing.

You cannot expect to know the detail of each facet in which you have an interest, a good network can guide you, but an adviser is needed to make knowledge relevants to point our the opportunities and steer you away from the pitfalls, which is why not only do you need an inner Ring of Confidence but you need a structure which allows you to manage them efficiently and well. We can tailor make a Protection Package with your inner Ring of Confidence in key roles, if you have not already got a suitable structure in place.

Educating the second generation to manage

There are two elements to preparing the next generation to inherit wealth; education and engagement.

1. Education

There are several training courses run by banks, training centres and consultants; some are good and some not. They depend very much on the experience of the trainer and what the trainer or sponsor wants to get out of it.

Care should be taken before a trainer is let loose on the second generation. You should know their goals and background. Clearly a bank wants to engage with the next generation so that on the death of the parents, or on the passing of wealth to the next generation, they will not take their business elsewhere. Some of these programmes are very good. There are others, however, where the trainer may be a trained psychologist or an academic, with no first-hand knowledge of the issues and concerns of the wealthy.

2. Engagement

This is by far the trickier aspect of the two. Jack is a founder of a vast business spanning many countries. He has children from three different mothers. The first mother, Susan, had two sons, John and George. George was a dynamo and Jack took care to engage him with the business. John was very much in George's shadow; he was a detail man but lacked common sense. George had it all; he was good looking, suave and much-loved.

Unfortunately, George died in a car crash which broke his father's heart. Then there came two further children, Charlotte and Harry, by another mother Jennifer. Jack spent less time engaging Harry and Charlotte in the business, but both went to university and ultimately into their father's business. Both were very good workers.

Harry showed a natural aptitude for the trade. Charlotte however, wanted to marry and to devote her time to her children. Harry was of course the natural successor. Jack then married for a third time to Laila and had a further two children, Damian and Olivia. They were very spoilt, saw school as optional and both were difficult.

Jack now has a problem. What is he going to do about John? Jack tried a number of options, putting him in control of a small outpost, but that did not work. Away from the watchful eye of his father, he soon began throwing his weight around and upsetting people. So Jack brought him back into the fold and put him in charge of a backwater group, but at head office. Jack found him annoying and eventually pensioned him off, which was when John began to decline. He took to drinking heavily, badmouthing his father, and generally keeping poor company.

With regard to Damian and Olivia, although still young, Harry has made it very clear that neither of his half siblings would ever have a place in the business and there would be no place for his stepmother either, who had been Jack's secretary.

Charlotte is fine, Harry loves her. But what is to happen to John, Damian, Olivia and Harry's stepmother when Jack is no longer around to look after them? All the money is tied up in the business and Jack cannot provide for them without access to the business. Although the business is ring-fenced from Harry's stepmother, I doubt whether that will stop her from litigating; she needs to provide for her children and will fight like an alley cat to do so.

Engaging the next generation is much trickier than would first appear. A company was left to four children, two boys, Geoffrey and Robert, and their sisters, Rose and Angela. The two boys were running the company and the two sisters were passive shareholders. Following the death of their father, Geoffrey and Robert continued to run the business but over time it appeared to run into difficulties and the share price tumbled.

Geoffrey and Robert called a shareholders' meeting. The sisters were told how badly the company was doing. Geoffrey and Robert offered to buy Rose and Angela's shares saying that they may as well get something for their shares while they still had some value. The two sisters sold their shares to their brothers. Within a couple of years the business was back to its former health and getting stronger by the day. The boys had deliberately run down the company to buy out their sisters on the cheap.

Family values are not always easy to instil

Families that focus from an early age on the culture of the family and the value of hard work can keep the family business together. For example Jennifer, Harry and Charlotte's mother, had integrity. She was honest and supported their father in every way. Although he went off with Laila, she remained a good mother to her children and a friend of her children's father. Her divorce settlement was probably less than she could have achieved if she had fought harder, but that was not of great importance to her at the time. What was important was bringing up her children well and preserving good relations.

> Families that focus on the importance of hard work and good family values can keep the family business together.

Looking at the unit of Jennifer, Harry and Charlotte, Harry will make sure Charlotte and his mother Jennifer are well looked after, but if viewed from a wider perspective, John, Damian and Olivia are not likely to fare so well. No matter how much Jack would like to instil family values of hard work and a united successful business, this scenario is bound to end in costly litigation, which will inevitably damage the business, possibly even destroy it.

A successful transition

To achieve a successful transition across the generations, you need a family that cares for each other and for the business. It must have real family values, few if any divorces, whopping good luck, and advisors who are not too self-interested. These values cannot be replicated, cannot be enforced, cannot be imposed and cannot be taught.

I was working for a family where the father, Maurice, insisted that his children work together for his charitable foundation. He had four children; Maureen, Hazel, Brin and James. While their father was alive they worked together on the foundation constitution and the areas of charitable endeavour they knew their father wanted.

However, on his death, the four children fell out. Their father had left them with little in the way of an inheritance, wanting them to work together for his foundation. Brin and James wanted to take out significant salaries for their work and Maureen and Hazel felt that was not what their father would have wanted.

In due course, they went to court to divide the foundation into two to allow Maureen and Hazel to run one half of the foundation as they thought fit and for Brin and James to run the other half.

Another family, one of the richest in the world, took a very different approach. Amin was a wise man with a family of three. Although he worked incredibly hard all his life, he'd always had time for his children and was a good father. He remained married to the same woman, to whom he was devoted.

Amin was adamant that whatever the tax consequences and advantages, on his death he wanted to divide his estate equally, leaving the businesses to the two boys, who were already running them, while giving an equal amount to his only daughter, to do with as she chose. One of his boys was into racing and was already spending a considerable amount of money on buying horses and stud farms. It was of no concern to the father that one of his sons may be squandering his money – his view was that his children could do with his money as they chose and work as hard or as little as they wanted. He did not think it was right to interfere.

Charitable giving is not all its cracked up to be

There are numerous celebrities and rich individuals who are applauded for giving substantial sums to charity. They have set up foundations to do so and are admired for being philanthropic.

However the reality is not so rosy. In 2013 £2.345 billion was given to charity. This would imply that this sizeable sum is being put to good use. In fact there is some £14.76 billion of undistributed funds. This would imply that donations are being made to a charitable foundation on which tax relief is claimed and then the monies are not distributed to where they are needed. This can be for a number of reasons. I have heard foundation boards say that the charities seeking their aid do not meet their requirements, that they want to preserve the capital and only spend the income to ensure longevity.

To my mind tax relief should only be granted when the funds are paid out for charitable purposes not for being retained and managed in a foundation.

A strong advisory board.

Advisory boards can be very useful provided they have the necessary skills and judgement and are not holding office for purely selfish reasons.

I have learnt many lessons about advisory boards, some more painful than others. Paul was not happy with his board of advisors. He had a new angel investment fund into which he had invested heavily, but it was still struggling to make ends meet. His advisory board appeared keen to assist. After the first meeting, Felix, who was the most outspoken on the board of six, suggested a splinter group of three be formed as a 'strategy' group. This strategy group did not seem interested in Paul's angel investment fund.

Paul had prepared an investment memorandum, but Felix paid only scant attention to it. Felix then suggested they meet Paul's contacts. They may wish to co-invest. After three meetings at which Paul introduced his contacts to his advisory board at his expense, Felix was making some seriously valuable introductions. Felix promised to pay Paul an introducer's fee on

> Advisory boards for charities are particularly prone to attracting individuals who are keen to meet the others on the board...

any investments that were made from Paul's contacts, but was reluctant to put anything in writing – it would be on a case-by-case basis.

Paul demanded that the advisory board pay some attention to his online angel investing fund; he was fed up with dishing out his contacts to Felix and the strategy board with little attention to his still struggling investment fund. Finally the other members of the advisory board began to see how self-interested Felix was and asked him to leave. Thereafter it worked well for Paul.

Wealthy families are often surrounded by the great and the good, which attract others. Care is needed that the people on the advisory board are in office to serve the best interests of the family and not their own selfish ends.

Advisory boards for charities are particularly prone to attracting individuals who are keen to meet the others on the board, but much less keen to introduce their friends and contacts to fundraising events and make donations to the cause.

Be circumspect when setting up an advisory board. You are allowing non-family members to get close, whether it be to your charity, trust, art collection, business or family. You must start only with a small group and test them out, each and every one. Make sure you do your due diligence: are they who they say they are? Don't just read their biography. Check that the companies for which they have claimed to work exist, and that the degrees they say they have are real. More importantly, what company do they keep? Birds of a feather flock together. If they habitually follow a culture of greed they will not keep good company, however if they operate from a culture of care, they will. Only offer an office on your advisory board to those who keep good company.

When members of the advisory board demonstrate care and prove that they are not driven by self interest then they need to be rewarded with a greater element of trust. But still keep the keys to the kingdom close to your chest, further down the line you may still need to sack them. Trusted advisors can become self-interested if the situation or their circumstances change, or the opportunity becomes too compelling. Keep your wits about you, your inner Ring of Confidence must be bound to serve your interests not their own.

Don't be intimidated by the envy of journalists and politicians

Most people think that the wealthy engage the best advisors to avoid tax, fly in private jets to swanky parties, and dine on slinky yachts amongst a star-studded cast. Being rich, as you know by now, is not really like that. Take Gary Barlow. He was mis-sold an Ice Breaker tax scheme and the journalists had a field day at his expense. It is not easy for the wealthy to know whether they are being mis-sold a dodgy tax product or a fabulous investment opportunity. The wealthy are a minority, so the press doesn't tell them about the danger signs that could alert them when they are at risk of doing something wrong.

> Nowadays good tax advice invariably increases your tax bill. But peace of mind is priceless.

Good tax advice, nowadays, rather than reducing your tax bill invariably increases it. One leading tax lawyer I know, says that more often than not when a UHNW individual has a tax review of his or her affairs or receives sound advice, they end up paying more tax than before – but can sleep at night knowing that HMRC will not be knocking on their door. A tax investigation is nasty with not only the tax to pay, but also the cost of legal representation and the potential for more tax and penalties. Peace of mind is priceless.

The top 1% of wealthy individuals in Britain pays 30% of the total income tax, its 104 billionaires spend £16 billion in the country, which equates to over £3 billion in VAT. Just seven boroughs in London account for one-third of all stamp duty raised, and Westminster and Chelsea raised £708 million last year.

It is the rich who drove the British economy out of recession and winched it out of the deepest recession it had known in 100 years.

It is often said that foreigners pay no tax in Britain. This is simply not true. The average non-dom pays £55,000, which is 22 times the national average. Their contribution helps pay for schools, police and hospitals, not just in London but across the whole country.

Today's rich, I am delighted to say, are now made up of normal people who have worked extraordinarily hard. John Caudwell grew up in poverty in Stoke on Trent, Duncan Ballantyne started selling ice creams from a van. Many people like to think that the rich make money from the exploitation of the poor, but as Howard Raymond, King of Soho, told me over lunch: "If you are selling a product that everyone wants to buy, who is exploiting whom?"

Journalists need to write stories that sell newspapers, and the rich and the mistakes they make are easy targets. If you have made some mistakes, it is probably wise to hire a PR agent to keep these stories out of the press.

Politicians also like to suggest policies that increase the taxes of the rich, or increase the ways in which they stop the rich from avoiding taxation, and to a large degree this has worked. The rich now pay more tax than others; it is not easy to avoid it, in the UK at least.

Final words

The UHNW community may not have the worries and concerns that the rest of us have; finding the resources to feed, clothe and house ourselves and our families. However, they have other issues and concerns. The rich, it is often forgotten, are human. They do not like being viewed with envy or taxed excessively because they have more money than others, neither do they like having their private lives made public by journalists keen on selling newspapers.

The truth is that they provide many of us with employment and contribute significantly to the countries which tax them. They can afford to be mobile, many have homes in other countries and plans in place to make alternative arrangements at the drop of a hat. If we want to benefit ourselves and the countries in which we live we should adopt a culture of care towards the UHNW individuals living in our community and be grateful for the contribution they make directly and indirectly to us all.

For more tips on how to build trusted advisor relationships, including helpful notes and videos please scan the code or copy the link **https://garnhamfos.squarespace.com/ wysr-extras/chapter-8-tips-and-notes**

Book Extras

We want you to get the most out of each of the Eight Chapters of this book *'When you are Super Rich Who Can You Trust?'*, so we have prepared special educational videos, helpful accompanying notes and questionnaires for each one.

If you wish to buy all eight with one FREE,
simply scan the code below or copy the link
http://www.garnhamfos.com/wysr-extras/
chapters-1-8-tips-and-notes

Turn to page 155 if you want to see how the accompanying notes and questionnaires can get you started in building your very own Ring of Confidence

Ring of Confidence

To fully enjoy your wealth, you need to be in control; but you cannot expect to be an expert in all the specialist areas which concern you, whether direct investment, smooth succession, tax mitigation or asset protection. You therefore need to find advisers you trust according to your list of interests and priorities – your inner Ring of Confidence, and a structure which gets the most out of them, our Protection Package.

If you would like to find out more:

Scan the code below or copy the link
http://www.garnhamfos.com

Contact Garnham Family Office Services for a consultation by scanning the code below or copying the link
http://www.garnhamfos.com/contact/

BConnect Club

Join our Exclusive Club for UHNW families to access relevant information on wealth preservation, vetted investment deals, luxury products and private events launched in October 2017. Membership for verified UHNW members is free.

Scan the code below or copy the link
http://www.bconnectclub.com

CPSIA information can be obtained
at www.ICGtesting.com
Printed in the USA
BVHW01s2318271117
501333BV00014B/633/P